THE OREGON TRAIL

MILESTONES
IN AMERICAN HISTORY

C 1

THE OREGON TRAIL

PATHWAY TO THE WEST

TIM MCNEESE

CHELSEA HOUSE
PUBLISHERS
An imprint of Infobase Publishing

The Oregon Trail

Chelsea House
An imprint of Infobase Publishing
132 West 31st Street
New York, NY 10001

Library of Congress Cataloging-in-Publication Data

McNeese, Tim.
  The Oregon Trail : pathway to the West / Tim McNeese.
     p. cm. — (Milestones in American history)
  Includes bibliographical references and index.
  ISBN 978-1-60413-027-0 (hardcover)
  1. Oregon National Historic Trail—History—Juvenile literature. 2. Overland journeys to the Pacific—Juvenile literature. 3. Pioneers—Oregon National Historic Trail—History—19th century—Juvenile literature. 4. Frontier and pioneer life—Oregon National Historic Trail—Juvenile literature. 5. West (U.S.)—Discovery and exploration—Juvenile literature. I. Title. II. Series.
  F597.M26 2009
  978'.02—dc22   2008030745

Chelsea House books are available at special discounts when purchased in bulk quantities for businesses, associations, institutions, or sales promotions. Please call our Special Sales Department in New York at (212) 967-8800 or (800) 322-8755.

You can find Chelsea House on the World Wide Web at http://www.chelseahouse.com

Series design by Erik Lindstrom
Cover design by Ben Peterson

Printed in the United States of America

Bang NMSG 10 9 8 7 6 5 4 3 2 1

This book is printed on acid-free paper.

All links and Web addresses were checked and verified to be correct at the time of publication. Because of the dynamic nature of the Web, some addresses and links may have changed since publication and may no longer be valid.

CONTENTS

Introduction

He was taking his new bride into the West, and she could not have been happier. The year was 1836. Marcus Whitman, from upstate New York, was a small-town doctor in his mid-thirties. He longed to become a missionary and minister to the Indian nations of the Oregon Country, the lands in the Far West that today make up the states of Oregon, Washington, and Idaho. He had read in the missionary press that American Indians were begging to learn about Christianity. They were pleading for salvation. Although the missionary journals exaggerated the Indians' desire for a new religion, pious Easterners such as Whitman believed that they represented the answer to the Indians' call.

RETURNING FROM THE WEST

Whitman had traveled west the previous year. He had gone on a fact-finding mission in the company of a Congregationalist minister more than 20 years his senior. He had walked the length of the great land route that ran from Missouri to Oregon's Columbia River, a distance of nearly 2,000 miles, and he had returned ready to go west to stay, all in the name of the Lord. He had met with the missions board, whose members had quizzed the physician about his intentions to migrate to the Far West and remain there as a medical missionary along with a wife. "Have you carefully ascertained," the board asked, "and weighed the difficulties in the way of conducting females to those remote and desolate regions and comfortably sustaining families there?"[1] The question was a reasonable one. No pioneer woman had ever traveled the length of the Oregon Trail.

The wife in question was a woman in her late twenties whom Whitman had courted before taking his first trip along the Oregon Trail. She was an energetic, pious New Yorker, and she burned with a zeal equal to that of her intended husband to minister to the western American Indians. Both Narcissa and Marcus Whitman were certain of their intentions to go west. They married on February 18, 1836. For their wedding, the bride wore a "bombazine dress of Puritan black which she had sewed together herself."[2] Narcissa may have chosen her wedding music with the couple's plans to leave immediately for the West in mind. At her wedding, she sang, in fine voice:

> Yes, my native land, I love thee,
> All thy scenes I love them well.
> Friends, connections, happy country,
> Now, I bid you all farewell.[3]

Although she wore black for her wedding, Narcissa purchased a small number of brighter print dresses for the trip west. She also bought a pair of small-sized men's boots to help her walk the trail when she wasn't riding a horse sidesaddle in proper,

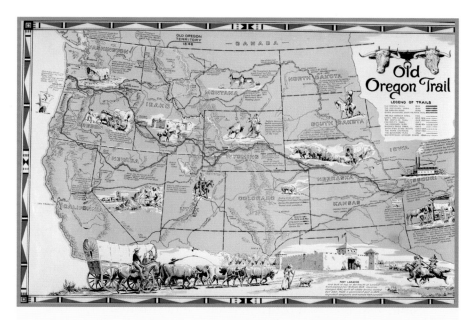

In 1843, the first emigrant wagon train made their first journey to unknown territory in the West. About 1,000 pioneers crossed the overland route called the Oregon Trail from the Missouri River to the Columbia River (from Missouri to Oregon), in what was dubbed the Great Migration.

ladylike fashion. She even planned to take along an inflatable life preserver for the many river crossings she knew lay ahead.

THE DIFFICULT TREK WEST

The Whitmans spent their honeymoon on the trail, in a tent that Narcissa had sewn together herself. It was fashioned out of striped bed ticking and waterproofed with oil. The newlyweds did not have the tent to themselves, however. They shared it with others who were prepared to take the Gospel to the western American Indians. These included another missionary couple, the sober-minded, hypercritical Henry Spalding and his "fragile, ineffectual wife, Eliza."[4] On the way west, Henry constantly tried the Whitmans' patience and nerves. Eliza Spalding, although serious and of determined courage, proved almost too weak for life on the trail. Prior to the couple's departure, she had given birth to a stillborn child. The tragedy left her physically and emotionally challenged.

The two couples met at Cincinnati, Ohio. From there, they set out by steamboat down the Ohio River to St. Louis and then up the Missouri River to Liberty, near modern-day Kansas City. There, Marcus Whitman bought a heavy farm wagon, one sturdy enough to carry the party's supplies and other items they would need to set up their Far West mission. He also purchased livestock, including a dozen horses, 6 mules, and 17 head of cattle, most of them milk cows. The Spaldings bought their own transport—a Dearborn—a light wagon decked out with yellow wheels.

Whitman had arranged for his group to attach itself to a fur-trading caravan under the direction of Tom Fitzpatrick, a fur trader and veteran of the trail. Without question, the inexperienced travelers had packed too much for their trek west. Their wagons were stuffed with unnecessary furniture, trunks of clothing, cases of religious material, a portable writing desk for Narcissa, and art supplies for Eliza.

Proceeding once more up the Missouri River, the Spaldings and Whitmans were joined by a fifth traveler, "thread-bare sixteen-year-old Miles Goodyear . . . from Iowa."[5] Trained as a carpenter, young Goodyear intended to become Goodyear the mountain man. The five emigrants caught up with Fitzpatrick's group in modern-day Bellevue, Nebraska, near the confluence of the Platte and Missouri rivers. As the Fitzpatrick caravan moved out along the Platte River, it "was one of the strangest ever to set off for the Rockies."[6] Among its numbers were approximately 70 assorted frontier–types. The group included American and French-Canadian fur trappers and several mixed-blood American Indians. Also in the caravan was a party of British sportsmen, led by Sir William Drummond Stewart, who were headed west to engage in a buffalo hunt. The British hunters were attended by servants and gunbearers. All now were followed by the missionary party, with their small herd of milk cows and calves.

HER PLACE ON THE TRAIL

Narcissa Whitman soon became a favorite of the men in the caravan. The novelty of having two women along caused some crude talk among the mountain men, which appalled Eliza. In contrast, "Narcissa glowed with exhilaration at the exciting adventure before her."[7] Raised in the household of a country judge, Narcissa was accustomed to profanity and did not chastise the men for it. In time, they gained her respect, and most of them tried to monitor their language around the women. Mrs. Whitman hosted tea parties, which the mountain men attended. Men who were used to drinking raw whiskey sat down and drank tea "brewed in a syrup can with water from a mountain stream."[8] Around evening campfires, the fur trappers regaled Narcissa, seated on her husband's knee, with stories of American Indians, close calls in the mountains, and other adventures. Marcus Whitman's wife became so popular that when the caravan's hunters returned with fresh meat, "the choicest cuts were brought to her tent and the bearer's canteen was always filled with fresh milk."[9]

Narcissa was enjoying herself. She took to the trail and found the experience thrilling. Every morning, she donned heavy men's boots and rode sidesaddle in her long, full skirts. In her diary she recorded the unique circumstances of the trail and described the party with which she was traveling. Every day brought something new. She was passing through the wilderness in a rough-and-ready caravan, but nothing seemed to faze her. Concerning a typical dinner on the trail, she wrote:

> Just take a peep at us while we are sitting at meals. Our table is the ground, our table cloth is an india rubber cloth, used

Narcissa Whitman (1808–1847) was the wife of Dr. Marcus Whitman, the first to lead a large party of wagons along the Oregon Trail. Very religious from a young age, the Whitmans answered the call for missionaries and would travel west to found the Whitman Mission in Oregon Country (which later became the state of Washington).

when it rains as a cloak; our dishes are made of tin—basins for tea cups, iron spoons and plates for each of us, and several pans for milk and to put our meat in when we wish to set it on the table—each one carries his own knife in his scabbard. Husband [her usual reference to her spouse] always provides my seat, and in a way that you would laugh to see us. It is the fashion of all this country to imitate the Turks. We take a blanket and lay down by the table.[10]

MORE TRAIL CHALLENGES

While Narcissa Whitman enjoyed life on the trail, Marcus Whitman appears to have had some troubles. She often wrote such lines as "Husband has had a tedious time with the wagon today."[11] The trek along the Platte River went well. Once the party reached the South Platte, however, and began to encounter the steeper rises that led to the Rockies, the missionaries' wagons could not keep up with the caravan. Marcus was compelled to throw out some of his heavier pieces of furniture. Past Scotts Bluff, on the western edge of Nebraska, the landscape became increasingly rugged, and the missionaries' animals became somewhat weakened. The Whitmans jettisoned more items that they once had thought essential to their planned mission work in the Far West.

By the time the party reached Fort Laramie, in modern-day Wyoming, Captain Fitzpatrick insisted that Whitman and Spalding abandon their wagons and load their cargo onto pack mules. Whitman resisted. Wagons had made the trip before, at least along a portion of the trail, and he was determined to take his all the way to the Columbia River. Fitzpatrick explained that such feats had been accomplished only by parties that had included enough men to practically build roads at places where none ran. Whitman finally agreed to give up his large wagon, but he convinced Fitzpatrick to allow the smaller Dearborn to continue on. The British buffalo hunters left the caravan at Fort Laramie and set out on their own in search of bison.

After Fort Laramie, the Oregon Trail became more difficult to pass along. The trail grew even more rugged as the caravan reached the eastern slope of the Rocky Mountains. Although

Fitzpatrick was in a hurry to make it to the mountain-man rendezvous at the trading post at the Green River in Wyoming, he stopped the caravan long enough for Narcissa and Eliza to climb a granite rock formation known as Independence Rock to write their names on it, as others did on the trail. The pack mules came in handy on this leg of the trek because they were able to press on nimbly at the rate of two or three miles per hour. For the remaining wagon, however, the path was not so easy:

> Trees had to be cut, boulders pried aside, and detours made around deep gulches. Often the wagon tipped over two or three times in a single day, and most of the load had to be thrown out or transferred to pack animals, but Whitman was as stubborn as impractical. While Narcissa and the Spaldings rode with the caravan, he and the unfortunate farmer and the carpenter fought the almost empty wagon up the valleys of the Platte and Sweetwater, and over South Pass to Bridger's Fort.[12]

Despite the difficulties, the poor battered Dearborn made it to the Far West trading post at the Green River.

Reaching the rendezvous site, the caravan joined a host of other mountain men and trappers, along with American Indians with whom they traded. For many of the men at the rendezvous, the sight of the pioneer women was a novelty. Some had not seen an American woman in several years. Inevitably, many men thought that Mrs. Whitman was a rare beauty. At the trading post, as on the trail, Narcissa made friends with a new group of western strangers. American Indian women "gathered in a throng, to touch their fingers to her white skin, marvel at her blue eyes, and admire her clothing."[13] As Narcissa wrote in her diary, "As soon as I alighted from my horse, I was met by a company of native women, one after the other, shaking hands and saluting me with a most hearty kiss."[14]

In respect and, perhaps, admiration for Mrs. Whitman, many of the mountain men at the rendezvous attended the morning and evening devotional services held by the missionaries. Narcissa and Eliza handed out Bibles and religious pamphlets and bemoaned that they had not brought more copies with them. "This is a cause worth living for!" Narcissa later wrote.[15]

At the rendezvous, the Whitmans and Spaldings met Nathaniel Jarvis Wyeth, a well-known trader in the Oregon Country. Wyeth had come into the region a few years earlier and established a trading post that he called Fort Hall, in what today is Idaho. He had sold the trading post to the Hudson's Bay Company, one of the largest and oldest fur companies in North America. Wyeth offered to write a letter on Marcus Whitman's behalf to introduce him to Thomas McKay, the director at Fort Hall. Wyeth told Whitman that he could attach his party to another group of traders and trappers that was scheduled to leave from Fort Hall for the Walla Walla region, in modern-day Washington State. Wyeth added, however, that Whitman would have to hurry to get to Fort Hall. To that end, Wyeth suggested to Whitman that he abandon the Dearborn. Again, stubbornly, the missionary refused. He was determined to blaze a wagon road to the Columbia River.

ASCENT AND DESCENT

Leaving the rendezvous site, the missionary party moved on, with the Dearborn in tow. Although Narcissa Whitman had enjoyed much of her experience on the trail during the previous months, she emerged from the Green River rendezvous disappointed, perhaps depressed. She had met some of her first American Indians and had been disillusioned. These people were not the figures of her imaginings, and her "romantic notions died hard."[16]

The trail became more difficult, and food became scarce. Narcissa grew homesick. "I thought of Mother's bread and butter many times as any hungry child would," she wrote. "I fancy pork and potatoes would relish extremely well."[17] Complicating things further, she was pregnant.

Marcus continued to obsess about his wagon, which Narcissa had long ago decided should simply be abandoned. She wrote repeatedly about the troubles he caused himself over the useless contraption: "Husband had a tedious time with the wagon today. Waggon was upset twice. Did not wonder at all this. It was a greater wonder that it was not turning a somerset [somersault] continually."[18] When an axle on the wagon broke near Soda Springs, in modern-day Idaho, she was certain the stubborn doctor finally would leave the Dearborn behind. Whitman simply "discarded the rear wheels and body, mounted a box on the front axle, and continued . . . to Fort Hall,"[19] however.

On reaching the fort, Narcissa Whitman and Eliza Spalding immediately were disappointed. The fort was very basic, even a bit run-down. The fort was cramped, and, as Narcissa wrote, "the vegetable garden had gone to seed."[20] The missionary party did arrive in time to join the caravan that Thomas McKay was leading to Walla Walla. McKay gave the missionaries and their animals the opportunity to rest for a few days and then set a course down the south rim of the Snake River Gorge.

For the formerly excited Narcissa, the long trail was becoming tedious and difficult, both physically and emotionally. She wrote in her diary: "Have six weeks steady journeying before us. Will the Lord give me patience to endure it. Long for rest but must not murmur."[21] For a while, the party lost the main trail and found itself wandering through low-lying swamps, where mosquitoes attacked the travelers in swarms. The group encountered sagebrush that stood three feet high, slowing them down further. At Salmon Falls, on the Snake River, Narcissa was greatly disappointed when her husband decided to abandon her trunk full of calico dresses, as well as her wedding dress.

"Poor little trunk," she wrote. "I am sorry to leave thee, thou must abide here alone."[22]

The caravan continued to be slowed by Whitman's useless ex-Dearborn cart. The contraption caused four mules nearly to drown when the cart's wheels and the mules' harness became entangled. McKay left three guides with the missionaries as he and his main party pressed ahead. At the Boise Basin, even the guides threatened to leave the missionaries behind if the Whitmans did not give up their cart. At long last, Marcus abandoned his whittled-down wagon. He was disappointed, but he had managed to prove one thing by his tenacity and stubbornness: A trekker could take a wagon along the full length of the Oregon Trail.

Without the encumbrance of the cart, the party made good time on the last leg of their journey. Nevertheless, the final weeks of the trek were miserable. Conditions caused Eliza Spalding to imagine that she would die before they reached their final destination. Despite the hardships, however, they moved faster than they ever had before. As the party passed along the slopes of the Blue Mountains, Narcissa Whitman was inspired by their peaks. She compared them to the Catskill Mountains of her native New York. It was here that she was able to wash her clothes for only the third time since the missionary party had left the Missouri frontier, three months and 1,500 miles earlier. They drove themselves onward. In her diary, Narcissa described how her husband's Indian horse was a "hard rider upon every gate [gait], except a gallop," a fact that led the party to proceed whenever possible at that swift pace.[23]

NEARING THE END

On August 29, 1836, the missionary party arrived at the 5,000-foot elevation of the mountains and could see Mount Hood in the distance, 200 miles away. That evening, Narcissa wrote, "just as we gained the highest elevation the sun was dipping his disk behind the western horizon."[24] Beyond the mountain landmark, Narcissa and the others knew that the Pacific Ocean was closer than ever, as was Fort Walla Walla. A couple of days before their arrival, the travelers spotted the fort in a valley. "You can better imagine our feelings this morning than we can describe them," Narcissa wrote in her diary, after Fort Walla Walla came into distant view. "We started while it was quite early, for all were in haste to reach the desired haven. If you could have seen us you would have been surprised for both man & beast appeared alike propelled by the same force. The whole company galloped almost all the way to the Fort."[25]

They reached Fort Walla Walla on September 1, 1836. Since leaving the Missouri River, they had traveled for just over six months. When they arrived within the fort's walls, their joy was complete. The fort was an 18-year-old trading complex and palisade that was owned by the Hudson's Bay Company. It was located in the southeast corner of the future state of Washington. After months of deprivation on the trail, the party at last sat down in cushioned chairs to enjoy a decent supper of pork, potatoes, melons, butter, and bread. Even the sound of a rooster crowing sent Narcissa into tears of joy.

The group wasted little time enjoying their arrival, however. The two missionary families set out immediately to establish themselves in their new missions. They built houses and other outbuildings in which to take up their work with the local American Indians. They did not work together, however. By the time of their arrival, the Whitmans and the Spaldings could not stand one another. The Spaldings chose to work with the Nez Perce Indians at Lapwai, or Butterfly Valley, in modern-day Idaho. During the next 11 years, the Whitmans worked with the Cayuse tribe. In the spring of 1837, Narcissa and Marcus Whitman brought their child into the world, a daughter whom they named Alice Clarissa.

The two families had endured a difficult trek across the Great Plains and the Rockies. The women, however, had

In 1836, Eliza Spalding and Narcissa Whitman became the first pioneer women to cross the Rocky Mountains. The journey was by sleigh, canal barge, wagon, river sternwheeler, horseback, and on foot. Their journey proved it was possible for women to travel overland, opening the way for several generations of emigrants to follow in their footsteps.

accomplished a unique success, another first on the trail. Narcissa Whitman and Eliza Spalding were the first pioneer women to travel the trail, cross the Rocky Mountains, and reach the Oregon Country overland. Nearly all who had traveled the trail in previous years—explorers, mountain men, fur traders, and missionaries—had declared the trail unfit for women and children. Now, however, two women had proven the skeptics wrong. Not immediately, but within a few short years, the Oregon Trail became the most heavily used trail crossing the American West. Endless trains of wagons lined the trail and delivered eager men, women, and children to lands that they hoped held promise and prosperity.

Traders and Trappers

For thousands of years, the Great Plains and the Rocky Mountains knew no trails other than those faintly carved by a wide assortment of prairie animals, including deer, elk, wolves, bears, and, of course, bison. The wildlife of the West cut game trails in almost every direction, routes made by nature and by nature's animal instincts: the shortest paths to food, to water, or to shelter. When the first humans reached North America, they followed these same trails in search of animals that could provide them with food. These early peoples of the Plains and the intermountain region also made their own paths, as they sought easy passes through the mountains. Between the animals and the American Indians, the first trails on the North American continent were well traveled before the first Europeans arrived, less than 500 years ago.

NEW ARRIVALS

When Europeans reached the northern lands of the Western Hemisphere, they, too, spread out on searches of their own. Explorers followed rivers and lakes into the interior. They found their way across the continent in search of fur, gold, and other riches. The vast interior lands of North America became the object of rivalries among various European powers. From the Great Lakes to the Rio Grande and from the Mississippi River of the Midwest to the Columbia River of the Pacific Northwest, British, French, Spanish, and even Russian explorers, traders, and fur trappers vied against one another to dominate one part or another of North America. From the 1600s through the 1700s, the West saw British traders, French voyageurs, Spanish fur trappers, and Russian explorers compete for supremacy.

With the arrival of a new century, the nineteenth, the curious people of yet another country reached into the West. They were citizens of a new nation, established just decades earlier. Their country was born in revolution and separation from Great Britain. They were the Americans, and their infant land stretched from the Atlantic Coast to the Mississippi River. They were looking beyond that great river, however, toward new lands just out of their reach. Soon, they arrived on the Great Plains. Then they looked further, to the lands beyond the Rocky Mountains.

With each passing decade of the nineteenth century, Americans showed increasing interest in various parts of the Far West. Although the Oregon Country had long been claimed not only by the British, but also by the Russians and the Spanish, many Americans now took a serious look in the direction of Oregon. Despite the Americans' interest, however, the non-Indian nation with the deepest roots in the Oregon Country in the early 1800s was Great Britain. British fur agents had arrived along the Columbia River during the 1700s, and the Hudson's

Bay Company had consolidated the British presence by establishing Fort Vancouver on the Columbia River.

AMERICANS REACH OREGON

Prior to 1800, few Americans had even seen Oregon. One who had was an American sea captain bound from Boston, a man named Robert Gray. He reached the Columbia River on May 11, 1792, and claimed the region for the United States. When Gray arrived at the mouth of the Columbia, he saw the river's entrance stretching for a distance of six miles across. He easily sailed his ship up the river a short distance and anchored. Before leaving, he named the river after his ship, the *Columbia*.

The American explorers Lewis and Clark reached Oregon during their expedition in 1805–1806. Their epic journey gave further legitimacy to an American claim to the region. The explorers and their military party of nearly three dozen encamped on the south bank of the Columbia through a long and miserable winter. For four months, it rained every day but eleven. When the Corps of Discovery, as the expedition was known officially, returned home, its participants told stories of their 28-month journey. These accounts included descriptions of the great Rocky Mountains, friendly and hostile American Indian nations, and an abundance of wildlife, especially fur-bearing animals such as beaver. Because beaver pelts were highly prized at the time, a generation of American fur trappers and traders soon made their way up the Missouri River into the Far West in search of the valuable animals. A permanent American outpost was set up in 1811 by a German-born New Yorker, fur entrepreneur John Jacob Astor.

The possibility of profiting from the western beaver trade had led Astor to dream of establishing a monopoly in the fur trade in the Oregon Country. He put together his American Fur Company and sent out two expeditions, each bound for Oregon. One expedition traveled by land; the other, by sea. In September 1810, a ship named the *Tonquin* left New York Harbor

The first American overland expedition to the Pacific Coast and back was led by Captain Meriwether Lewis and Second Lieutenant William Clark (*depicted above*). Also on the journey was Sacagawea, their Shoshone guide. The intent of the trip was to study American Indians, botany, geology, the Western terrain and wildlife, as well as to analyze the potential for commerce on the waterways in the region.

for the Pacific Coast. After months of sailing around South America, Astor's vessel reached the mouth of the Columbia. The crew soon began building Astor's trading fort, a log building dubbed Astoria, on the opposite side of the Columbia from the British Fort Vancouver. Ironically, after having completed a journey of thousands of miles, the ship *Tonquin* soon met with destruction. As Astor's trading post was under construction, the ship's captain sailed the *Tonquin* north to trade with American Indians. Off the coast of Canada's Vancouver Island, local American Indians attacked the ship. As the attackers boarded the vessel, a wounded crewman set fire to the powder magazine, the place below decks where gunpowder was stored. The resulting explosion blew the ship to pieces, killing everyone onboard. The loss of the *Tonquin* presented an immediate problem to the men back at Astoria. Perhaps, they hoped, the overland expedition that Astor had sent west would catch up with them.

That overland party had left St. Louis in March 1811. The leader of the expedition was Wilson Price Hunt. He had planned to take his party up the Missouri River, following the trail established by Lewis and Clark. Once he reached modern-day South Dakota, however, stories of the savagery of the Blackfoot Indians on the Upper Missouri caused him to abandon the river and set out overland. After crossing the Great Plains and the Rocky Mountains on horseback, Hunt and his party reached the Snake River. The men hacked out dugout canoes and set out down the river, through immense rapids. After weeks spent defying death on inland waters, they reached Astoria.

The rendezvous of the seagoing party and the overland party did not provide a substitute for the lost *Tonquin*, however. Somehow, contact would have to be made with Astor back in New York. Astor's partner-in-charge at the trading post, Duncan McDougall, decided to send a party of men back overland. The men were to carry official communiqués from Astoria and news of the latest turn of events. Ahead of them lay thousands of miles of western territory. To lead this return party, McDougall selected Robert Stuart, who had sailed on the *Tonquin*. (Fortunately for Stuart, he had remained at Astoria when the ship ventured north to its destruction.) Stuart, a 27-year-old Scot, was known for his resourcefulness and even temper. McDougall considered him a perfect choice for the difficult and dangerous trek back to the East.

HEADED BACK EAST

The Stuart party left Astoria toward the end of June 1812. In his journal, Stuart noted the day of departure: "In the Afternoon of Monday the 29th June 1812, 23 sailed from Astoria under a salute of cannon from the Fort."[1] Just as the overland party had paddled west in dugout canoes, Stuart and his men traveled east in canoes fashioned out of quarter-inch-thick cedar, held in place with brace boards that were tied together with a sturdy cord known as sturgeon twine. These small boats were waterproofed with gum. After two days of fighting against the current of the Columbia River, Stuart's party left the river. They gathered up all their goods, such as trade items, guns and ammunition, company papers, and personal gear, and traded for horses with a local American Indian nation. They then set out in a south-southeasterly direction into modern-day Idaho, then part of the Oregon Country.

Stuart and his men soon discovered that they had traded the difficulties of paddling up the Columbia River for a host of other problems. Off the river, they found that water was scarce. The summer heat was oppressive, and mosquitoes were a constant torment. Stuart's party pressed on, however. They encountered additional rivers along the way. By September, the mountain cold of autumn replaced the burning heat of the summer. Fortunately, the men stumbled into Shoshone country, where the American Indians "provided dog meat, dried salmon, and a flavorsome cake made of ground roots and serviceberries."[2] This was not the first time that the Shoshone people had been helpful to a party of Americans wandering across their lands. Seven years earlier, they had provided horses for the Lewis and Clark expedition.

Once the party left the Shoshone, they set off on foot in search of what was called the Indian Road, the route that one day would be known as the Oregon Trail. Progress on the trail did not come easy. On one late September morning, Stuart and his men woke up to the sound of their horses being stampeded by Crow Indians. Before the men could regain control of the animals, the American Indians had stolen all their horses. The situation was difficult. The men now were without horses, the mountains lay ahead of them, and winter was coming. Stuart and his party loaded their supplies onto their own backs and began to walk.

By the last week of October, the party found its advance blocked by a great ridge of the Wind River Mountains, a range of the Rockies in modern-day western Wyoming. These towering peaks stopped the struggling, half-starved men in their tracks. To advance farther seemed impossible. Stuart pushed ahead, however, until he found a way through the great Rocky Mountain barrier. He discovered a long, low pass through the mountains, one that his men could easily traverse. The pass could have accommodated horses or even wagons had Stuart and his men had either. In his journal, Stuart described what he saw before him: "Ahead the country in every direction south of east is a plain, bounded only by the horizon."[3] The intrepid Scot was not completely aware of the significance of his discovery beyond its immediate importance to his party. He had accidentally located South Pass, a route that, a generation later, took westward-bound wagon trains to their destinations in Oregon.

This broad pass opened up to the foothills of the Rockies and then to the western Great Plains. Stuart and his men reached the Sweetwater River and then the North Platte. The Missouri River lay ahead. By Friday, March 30, 1813, the Astor men had reentered American civilization, as noted in Stuart's journal: "We a little before sun set reached the Town of St. Louis, all in the most perfect health, after a voyage of ten months from Astoria."[4] Although Stuart's immediate mission had been to lead his men from the Pacific Coast back to the United States, he also accomplished something else in the process. Traveling from west to east, his party blazed the basic route of the Oregon Trail.

South Pass provides a natural crossing point of the Rocky Mountains and has been the route for several historical trails, including the Oregon and California trails. South Pass was known only to American Indians until 1812. In 1836 Narcissa Whitman and Eliza Spalding were the first non-American Indian women to cross the pass.

AMERICAN FUR TRADERS ON THE TRAIL

Although Stuart's success in finding a pass through the Rocky Mountains was important for future generations of Americans, his efforts did not lead to an immediate influx of pioneers onto the trail headed West. In the years following the War of 1812 [1812–1815], the Oregon Country still seemed far away, and the area was not yet officially American territory. (The trading fort of Astoria was captured by the British during the War of 1812.) Moreover, much of the land crossed by the Oregon Trail, primarily the vast grasslands of the Great Plains, was not considered habitable at the time. In 1806, U.S. Army explorer Lieutenant Zebulon Pike had trekked across the central lands of the Louisiana Purchase from Kansas to Colorado. He reported that the Great Plains were similar to "the sandy deserts of Africa" and suggested that Americans "leave the prairies, incapable of cultivation, to the wandering and uncivilized aborigines."[5] About six years after Robert Stuart traveled the Oregon Trail from east to west, Major Stephen H. Long of the U.S. Army Corps of Engineers led his own expedition of discovery across the central plains. As had Pike, Long described the lands he saw as little more than a "great American desert."[6] This confirmed in the minds of would-be American migrants that the Great Plains was a poor place to make a home. The Oregon Trail remained uncrossed except for bison herds and American Indians. The route blazed by Stuart and the Astor men was nearly forgotten.

For years, Great Britain and the United States could not agree even on the boundaries of the Oregon Country, much less on the issue of who "owned" the region. The British captured Fort Astoria, across the Columbia River from the British Fort Vancouver, during the War of 1812. They returned the fort to John Jacob Astor in 1818. Astor, however, was not immediately interested in retaking his old trading post. He wanted a guarantee from the U.S. Congress that they would provide him with a military force for protection. Congress did not do so, and Astor abandoned the fort. That same year, Great Britain and the United States agreed to occupy Oregon jointly. This gave the citizens of both nations the right to trade and to establish farms and other outposts in Oregon. The treaty was renewed in 1827.

Throughout the early decades of the 1800s, even as ship captains, fur trappers, and trading-post operators found their way to the Oregon Country, the region remained little known to many Americans. It was so remote, so far removed from the western borders of the United States, that the vast majority of the nation's citizens could not imagine moving there. Nor could they imagine a way to get there even if they wanted to. By the 1820s, however, a few imaginative Americans had their eyes on Oregon and were making plans.

During the 1820s, some American entrepreneurs rediscovered the advantages of the Oregon Trail. In the spring of 1822, a fur trade organizer, General William H. Ashley, advertised in a St. Louis newspaper for 100 young men to work as mountain men in the Far West. Ashley and his partner, Andrew Henry, intended to establish these employees as fur trappers in the Rocky Mountains. Beaver pelts would be their commodity. Among the men recruited through Ashley's ad was a 23-year-old hunter named Jedediah Smith. Smith was tall, dark haired, and religious. He carried a Bible with him at all times. He did not drink, smoke, or chew tobacco, and he refrained from profanity. He was a young man destined to make his mark on the American West and on the Oregon Trail.

Smith soon became one of Ashley's best mountain men. In September 1823, Ashley appointed Smith as an expedition leader and sent him with a party of 10 fur trappers out of Fort Kiowa, near modern-day Chamberlain, South Dakota. Smith's party went west along the White River, into the Black Hills, and then into the region of the Powder River. Smith was attacked by a grizzly bear along the way and nearly lost an ear; one of his partners, James Clyman, awkwardly sewed the ear back in place.

The men rode on across modern-day Wyoming to the foothills of the Wind River Mountains, where they encountered the Crow Indians. The Ashley men traded tobacco, glass beads, and trinkets for good-quality beaver pelts. The skins were so superior to the beaver that Smith and his men had found along the Missouri River that the Americans asked the Crow where they could find more like them. When the Crow indicated such beaver could be found farther west, Smith was discouraged. The Rocky Mountains lay directly in his path. The Crow, however, did not seem to understand exactly what Smith's concern

Jedediah Smith (1799–1831) was a hunter, trapper, fur trader, and explorer who is credited with traveling more extensively in unknown territory than any other mountain man. He is best known for leading a party of explorers who rediscovered South Pass and was recognized by the scar on his face from a grizzly bear attack.

was. To explain, Clyman "covered a buffalo robe with sand and scooped up several piles to represent mountains, then he 'walked' two fingers up and down."[7] Only then did the Crow chief understand the men's question: How can we get through the mountains? The chief changed the shape of the "mountains" that Clyman had made to indicate the existence of a low gap between two peaks in the Rockies—South Pass.

In late February 1824, after staying with the Crow during much of the winter, Smith and his men set out on horseback toward the mountains. They soon encountered harsh mountain storms that piled snow up in their path. They forced their way along the south branch of the Wind River and then reached the Sweetwater River. There, they met with a blizzard that nearly killed them. The Americans constructed makeshift shelters and lived on mountain sheep. Hunger continued to stalk them, however. By mid-March, they were on the move again, following the Sweetwater upriver. The mountains stood directly to the west. The Americans entered a gradually sloping area that stretched across 20 miles.

As they crossed the pass, which was largely free from snow, the men also crossed the Continental Divide, the high point of the Rockies that marks the eastward and westward flow of the continent's rivers. Once they emerged on the west side of South Pass, Smith and his men reached Big Sandy Creek. Breaking through the ice that sheathed the river, Smith realized that the river's waters flowed westward. Ashley's party of fur trappers had reached the same 7,550-foot-high pass that had been used by the Astor men a decade earlier. This time, however, South Pass was remembered.

WAGONS WEST

The following year, Jedediah Smith returned to South Pass. This time, he led a wagon party, the first train of wagons to pass along the Oregon Trail and through South Pass. Smith and some of his men had spent the winter in the Grand Tetons, trapping for beavers, while Clyman and several others from his party had delivered furs to Ashley in St. Louis. In June 1825, Ashley and Smith were reunited when Ashley delivered a supply-wagon train to the rendezvous at the Green River in Wyoming. Ashley needed a mountain partner to organize the next trapping season, and he offered the post to Smith. After only three years in Ashley's employ, Smith had been made a partner.

Smith returned to St. Louis with Ashley and organized a winter-supply pack train. He hired some new fur trappers and loaded his pack animals with $20,000 worth of trade items and supplies. Smith left St. Louis on October 30, 1825, with 70 new recruits and a herd of 160 horses. Another Ashley caravan was headed west, bound for the Oregon Trail. Along the way, Smith made a decision that affected future travelers along the trail. He shortened the route into a more direct one:

> Instead of following the left bank of the Missouri all the way up to the mouth of the Platte, he left the Missouri at its north bend and pushed westward briefly over the Santa Fe Trail to the mouth of the Kansas River. He forded the Kansas to reach the Little Blue, paralleled that stream past its headwaters, and went on to the Platte, about one hundred miles above its mouth. From there he went up the Platte to the Sweetwater, over South Pass, and down into the Green River drainage.[8]

The efforts of Ashley and Smith paid off in good profits in the beaver trade. By 1826, Ashley had made a small fortune. He sold out his share in the enterprise to Smith and two of his friends, William Sublette and David E. Jackson. Then, in 1830, Smith and his company made history once again on the Oregon Trail. This time, they did it with wagons.

Smith did not participate personally in putting together this wagon train bound for the Oregon Trail and the distant

Rocky Mountains. Despite his leading position in the company, Smith preferred to spend much of his time trapping and trading in the western mountains. It fell to Smith's partner, William Sublette, to organize the wagon party. The train included 10 wagons loaded with equipment and trade items. The advantage of taking wagons rather than pack mules or horses was that the traders did not have to unload their animals at the end of each day on the trail. The wagons that Smith and Sublette's men took on the trail in 1830 were smaller models than those that later made the Oregon Trail famous as a western wagon route. Each wagon was pulled by a team of five mules and was loaded with approximately 1,800 pounds of cargo. The Sublette train also took along a pair of Dearborns—small, four-wheeled wagons, each pulled by a single mule. The caravan also included 12 beef cattle and a milk cow.

The trip was not an easy one. The wagons swayed from side to side as they bounced along. River crossings were difficult. Only rarely did a riverbank slope gently down to the water's edge. Usually, the men of the train had to cut a bank back to water level to allow the wagons to approach at the level of the river. All of the wagons made the trip intact, however, and the caravan reached South Pass in approximately three months. For the first time, a train of wagons had reached the Rockies. As for the cattle, they were the first to arrive in the mountainous country.

DRUMMING UP SUPPORT

The following August, Smith led the return party back to St. Louis. Along the way, he made note of the improvements and changes that already had been made to the route of the Oregon Trail. A new fort, Fort Leavenworth, had been built to replace the smallish, indefensible Fort Atkinson. Slowly, Americans were pushing farther and farther up the Missouri River, leading the advance of migrants into the West. Not only were wagons

(continues on page 30)

MOUNTAIN MEN
AND THE RENDEZVOUS

The era of the mountain men in American history was short but colorful. They were, perhaps, the most multicultural group in the West: They included Frenchmen, Englishmen, Mexicans, Americans, American Indians, Scots—even Hawaiians. Western fur trappers were, perhaps, a breed unto themselves. They were a group of men, typically romanticized as free spirits, who made their livings by trapping and trading. At the center of their world were the fur-bearing animals of the West. Especially lucrative were beaver pelts. The fur was used to make the high-crowned hats favored by fashion-conscious men in such North American cities as Boston, New York, Montreal, and Quebec, as well as in the European capitals of London and Paris. The workdays of the mountain men were brutal. They set traps in icy mountain streams to attract their prey in the dead of winter, when the beavers' coats were thickest.

Although the mountain man often is considered the ultimate free soul of the West, nearly every mountain man worked for someone else. Most of the trappers were employed by one or another of a handful of western fur companies operated by British, Russian, Spanish (later Mexican), and American entrepreneurs. These companies included the British-operated Hudson's Bay Company, the Rocky Mountain Fur Company, and the American Fur Company. Company officials hired groups of mountain men and dispatched them into the Far West, where they typically worked in brigades. The trapping season lasted from fall to spring. At the end of each season, the fur companies hosted a gathering called a "rendezvous."

The fur trade rendezvous was held each summer from 1825 until 1840—the heyday years of the mountain men. Many of the gatherings were held in modern-day Wyoming, near the Green River. Before each trapping season, a place was designated for

the rendezvous. After the season, all the mountain men came to the chosen locale. They gathered along with American Indians who brought their furs as well. At the rendezvous, the trappers reported to the company officials for whom they worked, turned in their furs, got paid, and were resupplied for the next trapping season. One mountain man, Joe Meek, described a typical rendezvous:

> The lonely mountain valley was populated with the different camps. The Rocky Mountain and American companies with their separate camps . . . the Nez Perces and Flatheads . . . friends of the whites, had their lodges all along the streams; so that altogether there could not have been less than one thousand souls, and two or three thousand horses and mules.
>
> It was always chosen in some valley where there was grass for the animals and game for the camp. . . . The waving grass of the plain, variegated with wild flowers; the clear summer heavens flecked with white clouds that threw soft shadows . . . gay laughter and the murmuring of Indian voices, all made up a most spirited and enchanting picture.*

A rendezvous was a raucous gathering that also allowed mountain men to blow off steam following their difficult season of trapping. With so many mountain men and American Indians gathered in one place, there was a great deal of drinking, fighting, and general rowdiness. As one witness described a typical scene:

> The men drank together . . . they sang, they laughed, they whooped; they tried to out-brag and out-lie each other. Now and then, familiarity was pushed too far, and would effervesce into a

(continues)

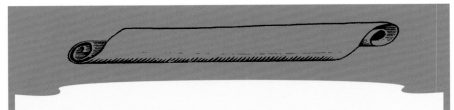

(continued)

brawl, and a "rough and tumble" fight; but it all ended in cordial reconciliation and maudlin endearment.**

The company officials who attended the annual rendezvous to collect the furs trapped by their employees and to sell them supplies brought those supplies from great distances, from places such as Fort Vancouver in the Oregon Country or St. Louis, back in Missouri. Those who traveled from St. Louis followed the Oregon Trail westward. One constant complaint of the mountain men who gathered at the annual rendezvous was the high cost of the goods they needed to purchase. A pound of beaver pelts was valued at about $4. With no other way of getting necessary items economically, a mountain man might pay, in furs, the equivalent of $4 for a pound of tobacco that cost pennies back in St. Louis. Red cloth that was used to trade with the Indians (it was popular with American Indian women) sold for $6 a yard. Whiskey sold for $4 a pint and usually was heavily watered down. In St. Louis, it was available for 15 cents a gallon. The end result of this lopsided economic system was that the typical mountain man spent most of the money he earned from a long trapping season at the rendezvous. This left him with little to show for his labor. It also meant that he had little choice but to go back to the same mountain streams he had worked the previous year and do it all over again.

---

* *Geoffrey Ward*, The West: An Illustrated History. *Boston: Little, Brown and Company, 1996, p. 61.*
***Ibid.*

(continued from page 27)
going west, but small steamboats also were finding their way up the Missouri River. Such boats were popular because they allowed migrants to "lop off 250 miles of slow, boggy road

travel between St. Louis and Independence, Missouri."[9] Independence remained a popular starting point for the land trail, but other towns, such as Westport, Missouri, also gained in importance.

The gains and inroads made by Jedediah Smith, William Sublette, and others led Smith and Sublette to write to U.S. Secretary of War John H. Eaton. They informed him that although they had taken wagons only to the Rocky Mountains because their company's annual trade rendezvous was held along the eastern slope of the Wind River, wagons could be taken along the Oregon Trail all the way to Oregon. It would remain for the next generation of Americans to do so, however.

New Pioneers on the Trail

Wagons had made their way to the shadow of the Rocky Mountains. Regarding the potential of the Oregon Trail, during the 1820s, Jedediah Smith accomplished more than any other American. Smith was a mountain man and a fur trapper, however. He was not a migration promoter. His encouragement of wagons on the Oregon Trail had value to him only inasmuch as it might improve his and his company's efforts in the western fur trade. Furthermore, wagons had not yet made their way along the Oregon Trail to Oregon itself. Although Smith had made significant contributions, it remained for others to add their own efforts toward making the Oregon Trail a practical route for a larger number of Americans.

THE FRENCH CAPTAIN
Within two years of Sublette's delivering wagons to Smith's company rendezvous, another would-be westerner prepared to

Benjamin de Bonneville (1793–1878) was a noted explorer who served in the Federal Army during the American Civil War. In 1832, Bonneville and a caravan of 110 men and 20 wagons was the first group to take wagons over South Pass.

make his mark on the history of the Oregon Trail. Once again, St. Louis was the center of attention. After years of service on the frontier at posts in the Arkansas Territory (today's Arkansas and Oklahoma), U.S. Army captain Benjamin Louis Eulalie de Bonneville was granted a leave of absence. His new personal goal was to become a major competitor in the western fur trade. Bonneville's plans included hauling trade goods and furs by wagon along the entire length of the Oregon Trail, all the way to the Columbia River and the Pacific Coast.

The 36-year-old, French-born Bonneville had spent years with the army, posted out on the Great Plains. He understood the difficulties of western travel. He was fully aware that any attempt to take wagons from one end of the trail to the other, a trip that would involve taking them across the Rocky Mountains, was a gamble. He soon solidified his plans and hired two associates, Michael Cerre and Joseph Reddeford Walker, both seasoned mountain men.

Bonneville and his party set out from Fort Osage, a frontier post located east of modern-day Kansas City, Missouri. Accompanying Bonneville, Cerre, and Walker were more than 100 men and 20 wagons that rolled along the prairie in two parallel lines. Mules, horses, and even oxen pulled the wagons. Oxen—castrated bulls—had been used for years to pull wagons back East and along the Santa Fe Trail. In 1832, however, they were new to the Oregon Trail.

As Bonneville's party moved away from Fort Osage, the men and animals settled into a routine. At the end of each day of travel, the wagons were moved into a square formation, with a distance of 30 feet between wagons. This square was closed in by chains and ropes that connected the wagons. The animals were herded inside the great wagon square to protect them from American Indians and prevent them from stampeding. Several men hunted for the party, finding plentiful game along the banks of rivers.

In less than two weeks, the Bonneville party reached the Kansas River. During the two weeks that followed, the men

Crossing the rivers was difficult and dangerous. If the river was shallow and not moving fast, travelers could cross by fording (crossing at a safe place). For deeper waters, they would build a large flat boat called a scow, and the animals would have to swim across. At times it could take up to five days for an entire wagon train to cross a river. Pictured are emigrants fording the Platte River.

continued on across the treeless plains of eastern Kansas, where the game ran short at times and the temperatures reached into the nineties, even though it was only late May. By June 2, the party reached modern-day Nebraska and the banks of the Platte River, which the men hailed as "the coasts of Nebraska!"[1] The Platte proved to be a formidable challenge for the wagon party. At some places, the river was as wide as one to three miles, but only a few feet deep. The problem was the unsettled river bottom. It was composed of shifting sands and mud that made fording the river extremely difficult and even dangerous for the wagons.

Bonneville and his men followed the Platte's south bank, looking for a possible crossing. Finally, at the fork of the South and North Platte rivers, Bonneville ordered the wagons' wheels taken off and the wagons made waterproof. This was done by covering the wagon boxes with buffalo hides and sealing them with animal tallow and ashes. The wagon men then became river men. Three men boarded each wagon box and floated it across the river, steering with poles as others pushed the wagons along the South Platte to its north bank. Once the wagons were ashore, the wheels were replaced and the wagons were rolled to the banks of the North Platte. The animals presented an additional problem, especially the mules. The mules' small hooves sank easily into the soft and shifting sands of the rivers. The men also learned that, if a mule ever got water in its ears, the animal would panic. Sometimes a panicked animal might even die.

ALONG THE PLATTE

With river crossings behind it for the moment, the Bonneville wagon train continued westward. The caravan stayed in close proximity to the North Platte. The cottonwood trees that were plentiful in the river bottoms provided firewood. Wild game was abundant. Evenings were spent around a comforting fire, with the livestock corralled and the wagons in a square. The Nebraska plains soon gave way to rolling hills and high bluffs, however—a signal of changes in the landscape. The party passed a rock formation that later became known as a marking post along the Oregon Trail: Subsequent travelers named this thin, 400-foot-tall shaft of limestone Chimney Rock. At this point, the party had traveled 550 miles from Fort Osage. Farther along the way, the wagon train reached Scotts Bluff. Along the bluffs in the area, the men shot mountain bighorn sheep for food.

In late June, the Bonneville party had an encounter with 60 Crow warriors. The Crow swooped down on the wagon train, causing a general panic. Bonneville's men struggled to circle their wagons into a defensible formation. At the last moment, the Crow turned their horses. They had merely intended to show off their horsemanship to the travelers. Only after Bonneville sat down with the Crow chief to share a ceremonial smoking pipe, did the former army officer and his men realize that the Crow had been shadowing them for several days.

The Crow finally departed, and the wagon caravan proceeded once again. The party had reached the eastern portion of modern-day Wyoming, where "the dry air was easy to breathe and fragrant with sage, but it shrank the woodwork on the wagon boxes and the spokes on the wheels."[2] All along this hilly country, the landscape was broken up by ravines and gullies. This made progress for the wagon train slow. Stones along the trail damaged the horses' hooves.

By mid-July, the Bonneville party left the banks of the North Platte and crossed two days' worth of sandy ground until they reached the Sweetwater River. Ahead of them lay the Rockies. On July 20, the men reached the Wind River Mountains. The wagons had taken a beating during the long months of travel. Several were about to fall apart. Wagon wheels were an immediate problem, and the men came up with a makeshift solution:

> [S]omething had to be done about the wheels or the train would grind to a permanent halt. A drastic remedy was tried: the iron tires were taken off, bands of wood nailed around the outside of the felloes [rims], the tires heated and replaced, and the whole dropped into cold water. The hot iron contracted rapidly against the moisture-swollen wood, and the wheels were sturdy again.[3]

Continuing onward, the wagon party reached the eastern slope of South Pass by late July. This marked the first time that wagons had crossed the Continental Divide. On July 27, Bonneville informed his men that they had reached the Green River—the end of their journey. Once again, wagons had passed along the Oregon Trail into South Pass and were on the verge of the Oregon Country.

Bonneville soon set up shop in a makeshift log fort. He sent his trappers out and readied himself to trade with the American Indians and make his fortune in the western fur business. Success in the fur business was not to be his, however. John Jacob Astor's firm, the American Fur Company, was already trading nearby, and Astor's men proved to be formidable rivals. At every turn, Bonneville was thwarted, as Astor's trappers and traders kept much of their own business and even managed to steal away some of Bonneville's men. By 1835, the intrepid Bonneville was broke.

Bonneville did succeed at something else in the West, however. From his trading post, he was able to observe the comings and goings of hundreds of mountain men and fur traders. Many of them were not American, but British. Although Bonneville did not take his wagons into the Oregon Country, his trappers ventured into the region. From Oregon, the trappers fed information back to Bonneville, who then wrote reports back to officials in Washington City, the nation's capital. For all practical purposes, Bonneville operated along the Oregon Trail as an American intelligence agent.

Following his bankruptcy, Bonneville emerged a success in other ways. In 1837, a book was published that described his adventures. The author was a well-known writer of popular fiction named Washington Irving. Irving's works included such tales as *Rip Van Winkle* and *The Legend of Sleepy Hollow*. His book *The Adventures of Captain Bonneville* made Benjamin Bonneville famous. Irving's book had other results, too. It caused many Americans finally to take serious notice of Oregon, that place so far away on the other side of the continent. The public—including newspapermen, migration promoters, and members of Congress—began to ask whether the time had come to end the United States's joint occupation, with the British, of Oregon.

MOUNTAIN MEN AND MISSIONARIES

In 1833, the *Christian Advocate and Journal,* a Protestant religious publication, printed a letter in one of its issues. The letter was an impassioned plea from a recent convert to Methodism who was part American Indian. The writer claimed that four American Indians from the Far West—three Nez Perce and one Flathead—had made a visit to St. Louis in 1831, in search of a book. These four American Indian chiefs had traveled 3,000 miles to locate the book that they described as the "white man's Book of Heaven."[4]

The book the chiefs sought was, of course, the Bible, which they believed represented great power or medicine. The letter went on to state that this visitation by the four leaders indicated that the tribes of the West were seeking, hungrily, to convert to the white man's religion. They were in search of Christianity. Should not good Christians, therefore, meet the challenge by taking up their crosses and heading west to spread the Gospel to the "heathen nations" of American Indians?

It is doubtful that the American Indians described in the letter had a true understanding of Christianity or that they actually sought to convert from their own native beliefs. It is more likely that they had heard about Christianity, God, the Bible, and Jesus Christ from fur trappers and traders and had "gained the idea that the white man's power was centered in his religion."[5] Even the American Indians' concept of power probably was misunderstood by the letter writer. The power that the American Indians associated with their white contacts was in the goods for which they traded. If obtaining the "Book of Heaven" meant that they would become richer in guns, blankets, metal tools, and beads, these four American Indian leaders were prepared to travel across the continent to obtain it.

Unfortunately, the chiefs' visit to St. Louis did not produce many positive results. Following meetings with the federal government's superintendent of Indian affairs, General William Clark (of Lewis and Clark fame) and several Catholic priests, two of the chiefs died of disease and exhaustion. A third died on a steamboat headed back up the Missouri River. The fourth chief reached the Nez Perce village in modern-day Montana. He informed his people that whites would arrive soon, bringing with them the coveted "Black Book." He, too, died soon, killed by Blackfoot Indians. Taken altogether, this was a story of tragedy, of a search for salvation, and of inspiration. The letter in the Protestant journal touched the spiritual hearts of untold numbers of zealous Christians. Some of them began making plans to bring the Gospel to the American Indians of the West.

HALL JACKSON KELLEY
(1790–1874)

The Fateful Trip West

Hall Jackson Kelley, the Boston schoolteacher who introduced Sunday school to his city, dreamed for years of leading a party of New England immigrants to the promised land of the Oregon Country. Even after many delays and the collapse of his immigration group, the American Society for Encouraging the Settlement of the Oregon Territory, Kelley held onto his dream. Eventually, after more than 10 years of planning, he set out for the West. The year was 1833.

With no followers remaining to share his vision, Kelley set out virtually on his own. Moreover, when he finally made his move westward, he did not travel to Oregon on the overland trail. He took passage, instead, on a ship that sailed down to the coast of Mexico. He crossed overland in Mexico and then wandered his way northward into California. When he reached the city of Monterey, he joined a party of horse traders who were set to drive a herd of horses and mules north to Fort Vancouver. The timing was perfect. Kelley would

ORGANIZER HALL JACKSON KELLEY

The call, in 1833, to send missionaries into the remote corners of the American West was not a new one. One of the earliest advocates of such endeavors was a Boston schoolteacher named Hall Jackson Kelley. Kelley had been instrumental in establishing the first Sunday school in the city of Boston. (He had also introduced the first blackboard to the city's public schools.) In 1824, years before the four American Indian visitors were to reach St. Louis, Kelley called on Protestant groups to take the message of Christianity to the western American Indian

have companions on the last leg of his journey into the Oregon Country that he had dreamed of for so many years.

Everything did not go well on this final segment of his trip, however. Along the way, the party came upon a small group of men who requested permission to join them, just as Kelley had done. Unfortunately, these new members of the group were horse thieves, on the run from California officials. When the party reached Fort Vancouver, word of the thieves already had reached the fort. Everyone in Kelley's group of horse traders was assumed to be a horse thief. Kelley managed to explain himself and eventually was cleared of any wrongdoing. The arrival into the Oregon Country that he had imagined for so long was marred, however. Kelley was a disappointed man. He wandered around Oregon but found little direction for himself. Not long after arriving, he decided to leave Oregon. He took a ship back to Boston, where he remained for the rest of his life. The Oregon dreamer was finished with his dream. In 1874, he died alone and in poverty, a forgotten man.

nations. He had quit his teaching job the previous year to work on the missionary project full time.

No man could have seemed more certain of his mission in life than Hall Jackson Kelley. He was certain that he had received a calling directly from God. He wrote, "The word came expressly to me to promote the propagation of Christianity in the dark and cruel places about the shores of the Pacific."[6] In time, Kelley's dream of Christian missionaries dispatched to the Far West to preach to the American Indians included a plan to establish a colony of 3,000 New Englanders on the banks of Oregon's Columbia River. There, the transplanted Americans would build a community of believers who would farm the land, build sturdy houses and churches, and convert the American Indians, just as he had planned from the beginning.

Kelley's efforts did not immediately bear fruit. He wrote and published promotional tracts that described the advantages to be had in Oregon. It was, he said, a place rich in timber and teeming with beaver and salmon. The land was so fertile and ripe that "the production of vegetables, grain, and cattle will require comparatively but little labor."[7] Through dedicated planning, by 1829, Kelley had convinced 500 Oregon advocates to form the American Society for Encouraging the Settlement of the Oregon Territory. The organization's mission statement declared its support for "planting, in the genial soil of those regions, the vine of Christianity, and the germ of Civil Freedom."[8] Kelley's group talked about packing their worldly possessions and moving to Oregon, but they never actually took the steps to do so. For one member of the society, the constant delays became unacceptable. By March 1832, a 29-year-old Boston businessman named Nathaniel Jarvis Wyeth, finally walked away from Kelley's organization with plans of his own.

New Missions
in Oregon

Nathaniel Wyeth was a man of vision. When he was not yet 30, he made money by cutting winter ice out of New England ponds and delivering it by ship to the sultry ports of the West Indies. Hall Jackson Kelley's call for immigration and missionary work in Oregon inspired Wyeth, but the Kelley group's indecision and failure to take even the first step beyond planning drove Wyeth to take up the cause of Oregon migration as his own. Like Kelley, Wyeth recruited willing colonizers. In a short time, he had 20 followers, whom he described as "industrious and temperate men."[1] Among them were a 19-year-old cousin named John Wyeth, and Jacob Wyeth, a Boston physician. Other recruits included a gunsmith, a blacksmith, a pair of carpenters, two fishermen, several unskilled laborers, and a group of farmers.

WESTWARD WYETH AND WAGONS

Wyeth planned all of the details necessary for his group to make its way west along the Oregon Trail to the Pacific Northwest. He ordered three wagons shaped like gondolas that could be used for river crossings. He bought equipment, tools, and weapons, including muskets, bayonets, and knives. He ordered uniforms for his men, matching outfits that included "pantaloons, striped shirts and cowhide boots."[2] Before the group left for Oregon, Wyeth whipped his men into shape for the rigors of the western trail by taking them to an island in Boston Harbor for physical training. In March 1832, with everything planned and prepared, Wyeth and his followers set sail for Baltimore. There, they added four more colonists to their number.

Things soon began to fall apart for Wyeth, however. He was warned that his boat-wagons were not sturdy enough to withstand the rugged western landscapes, so he traded them for new ones, losing money in the process. Even before his party reached the jumping off place for the trail at Independence, Missouri, six of his men quit the group, fearful of the American Indians they might encounter. Fortunately, Wyeth was able to attach his group of greenhorn easterners to a party of fur trappers headed west. The trappers were led by William Sublette, by now a veteran of the Oregon Trail and the challenges of the fur trade. Sublette was just the man Wyeth and his inexperienced party needed. Wyeth's cousin John wrote in his journal, "We must have perished for want of sustenance in the deserts of the Missouri had we been by ourselves."[3]

The trail proved to be a challenge for the Wyeth party. Wyeth's men did manage to make it to Pierre's Hole, Wyoming, by July 1832, before seven more members of the party quit. Those who quit included Wyeth's cousin John and his brother Jacob. The men who chose to turn back accompanied Sublette on his return to St. Louis. When that party was attacked by Blackfoot Indians, seven mountain men and one of Wyeth's followers were killed.

The first section of the Oregon Trail bisected two American Indian tribes: the Cheyenne and the Pawnee. The American Indians were quite sympathetic: helping to pull out stuck wagons, rescuing drowning emigrants, and even rounding up lost cattle. A common misconception is that American Indian tribes were the biggest threat to the emigrants. This painting is called *The Attack on the Emigrant Train.*

Nathaniel Wyeth continued to push on toward Oregon. His efforts were rewarded when he reached Fort Vancouver, the primary regional fur post of the Hudson's Bay Company. The date was October 29, 1832. His arrival in Oregon was a singular victory and a milestone for the western trail. Wyeth was the first to successfully lead a party of immigrants with wagons across the Oregon Trail. There were other victories, as well, from Wyeth's efforts. One member of his party, a lawyer named John Ball, soon opened a school to teach American Indian children of mixed blood. It was the first school established in Oregon. Others in Wyeth's group established farms along the Willamette Valley, thereby becoming the first permanent immigrant residents of the Oregon Country.

The 1832 trek was not Wyeth's one and only time on the Oregon Trail. After spending the winter of 1832–1833 in Oregon, he set out on the trail again, headed back East with plans to return with another party of immigrants. To cover his expenses, Wyeth received a contract at the 1833 trappers' rendezvous to bring supplies back the following year. Returning to Boston as a successful immigration organizer, Wyeth began to recruit for his second overland venture, set for the spring of 1834.

LEE'S CONTRIBUTION

Wyeth's second party included a 31-year-old Methodist minister named Jason Lee. Lee soon made his mark on the Oregon Trail. He had seen the letter in the *Christian Advocate*, and he was interested in helping to convert western American Indians. Lee was a good recruit for Wyeth's immigrant party. He was a tall, well-built, energetic young man who had grown up farming and was used to hard work. Friends claimed that he was strong enough to "chop a cord of wood in two hours."[4] As for his spiritual skills, Boston's Methodist bishop described Lee's piety as running "deep and uniform."[5] After Lee recruited his nephew, Daniel Lee, to Wyeth's party, Wyeth and the Lees went out and campaigned for contributions to encourage missionary efforts in Oregon. By spring 1834, the party included Wyeth, the two Lees, and two scientists, Thomas Nuttall and John Kirk Townsend. Nuttall, an Englishman, was one of the most famous botanists in America at the time. He had helped to catalog the plant specimens brought back by the Lewis and Clark Expedition. To enhance his missionary efforts, Jason Lee also brought along a schoolteacher and a pair of assistants. Wyeth's group finally numbered approximately 70 members in all. The party set out for the West in late April 1834.

Wyeth's second venture along the trail again included wagons. For the most part, these were filled with the supplies that he had contracted to deliver to the trappers. Everything went well until the party reached Pierre's Hole in Wyoming. Only then did Wyeth find out that William Sublette, his old comrade, already had provided supplies to the mountain men in the region. Wyeth pressed on toward Oregon. Along the Green River, the party met Thomas Fitzpatrick, one of the trail's pathfinders, who accompanied them to the annual rendezvous. There, Wyeth's group encountered the mountain men and American Indians who regularly traded and trapped beaver with one another. Present at the rendezvous were several of the most noted trappers of the day, including Jim Bridger, Kit Carson, and the Scotsman Captain William Drummond Stewart. Stewart agreed to accompany Wyeth's party out to Oregon.

Heading farther west, the Wyeth party crossed the Rockies. With his wagons of extra supplies, Wyeth established a trading post along the Snake River in modern-day southern Idaho. He dubbed the post Fort Hall, after one of his financial supporters. A homemade American flag of "bleached sheeting, a little red flannel, and a few blue patches," was hoisted over the fort.[6] Fort Hall did not prove to be a success because of the fur trade, however. The beaver-fur business was beginning to run down. European and American East Coast fashion had shifted to silk hats, with the result that beaver pelts were not as much in demand as in earlier years. The beaver populations in many places had been trapped out, as well. As the years went on, Wyeth's fort found its greatest value as a stopping place along the Oregon Trail for wagon trains of Oregon-bound immigrant families.

It was here that Jason Lee saw some of his first Flathead Indians, a group that the *Christian Advocate* letter had spoken of. Lee was disappointed at what he saw. He wrote, "The Indians play foot-ball on Sunday, and (tell it not to Christendom) it has been taught them by people, calling themselves Christian, as a religious exercise."[7]

Wyeth's party and the Lees continued on their way to the Columbia River and finally reached Fort Vancouver. It was there that the party found Hall Jackson Kelley, the man who had originally inspired Wyeth to go to Oregon. Kelley was not well. He was struggling with fever and on the verge of leaving the region entirely.

FOUNDING A MISSION

At the fort, Jason Lee was greeted by the regional director of the Hudson's Bay Company, Quebec-born Dr. John McLoughlin. From this friendly Canadian administrator, Lee learned that the Flathead Indians lived hundreds of miles to the east, in hostile territory. McLoughlin advised the newly arrived Methodist minister to settle along the Willamette River Valley and leave the Flatheads to themselves. In the valley, Lee and his associates could minister to another American Indian nation, the Callapoewah. Lee and his friends followed McLoughlin's advice. They paddled 60 miles up the Willamette River until they reached settlements that included "farms, flocks, sawmills, and orchards established largely by Americans who had arrived by the sea route."[8] They chose a spot on the river's east bank, among a grove of oak and fir trees. After a month, with winter just around the corner, the missionary party built a cabin.

By February 1835, Jason Lee was busy writing letters to the Methodist Mission Board back in Boston, asking them to send more missionaries. The mission needed more men, he wrote, as well as complete family units. Women would be a great asset, wrote Lee: "White females would be of the greatest importance to the mission, and would have far more influence among Indians than males."[9] To that point in time, however, no immigrant woman had yet endured the hardships of the Oregon Trail. In his letters to the mission board, Lee also requested farm equipment, seeds, and young fruit trees to add to the valley's existing orchards.

During the following two years, the Methodist board took its time in responding. Meanwhile, Lee and his associates farmed, grew fruit trees, and operated their mission school, which was attended by several American Indian and mixed-blood children. By May 1837, Methodist reinforcements arrived by ship. These new immigrants included 13 men, women, and children. Three of the women were single, and one of them, New Yorker Anna Maria Pittman, married Jason Lee just two months after her arrival in the Oregon Country. Theirs was the first Christian marriage ceremony in Oregon. Lee continued to serve as a great promoter of immigration to the Oregon Country in the years that followed. He eventually lost his church post because he spent too much time on immigration and not enough on mission work.

WHITMAN ON THE TRAIL

Although the Methodists were among the first Christian churches to respond to the clarion call of the *Christian Advocate* to convert the western American Indians, other groups also contributed their own efforts. These others included the Congregationalists and the Presbyterians. One who heard the call was a small-town doctor from upstate New York, Marcus Whitman. Even though he had trained as a physician, the 34-year-old Whitman had grown up believing that he had a call to the ministry. Whitman's family had not had enough money to afford the seven years of training required by the local Congregationalist church to become an ordained minister. Because medical school was cheaper and required fewer years of training, Whitman became a doctor. He also taught Sunday school and gave talks on the evils of alcohol.

In 1834, Whitman applied to the American Board of Foreign Missions in Boston to take up ministry in Oregon,

On May 25, 1836, Marcus Whitman (1802–1847) and his wife, along with a group of missionaries, joined a caravan of fur traders traveling west. In 1843, he traveled east, and on his return he led the first large group of wagon trains west from eastern Idaho. Called the Great Migration, it established the viability of the Oregon Trail for later travelers.

where he could serve as "physician, teacher, or agriculturalist."[10] The board had already enlisted the talents of the 55-year-old Reverend Samuel Parker. Parker had read the *Christian Advocate* Indian letter but had not moved quickly enough to accompany the Lees westward. The board assigned the enthusiastic Whitman to accompany Parker on a fact-finding mission to Oregon. (Although Whitman was a Presbyterian, the missions board was operated by both Congregationalists and Presbyterians.) Before he left for the West, Whitman began to court a young woman from the neighboring town of Prattsburg. Narcissa Prentiss was "pretty, vivacious, deeply religious, and ideally talented for a frontier missionary's wife."[11] This courtship was crucial to Whitman's plans to take up mission work in the West: The missions board required that he be married before it would sponsor him officially.

Parker and Whitman set out together and reached St. Louis in April 1835. They subsequently departed from Liberty, Missouri, along with fur trappers and traders in the employ of the American Fur Company. The fur men did not like the missionaries. They considered them to be "meddlesome do-gooders."[12] The mountain men made their animosity clear to the ministers. "Very evident tokens," wrote Whitman, "gave us to understand that our company was not agreeable, such as the throwing of rotten eggs at me."[13]

Whitman soon proved himself to the other men in their party, however. About a month out on the trail, a member of the group came down with cholera, a disease that often kills in less than a day. Others also became ill, including the party's leader, Lucien Fontenelle. For nearly two weeks, Whitman tended the sick and dying. In all, three men died. Those who survived admired Whitman's heroic efforts in tending the sick. Fontenelle changed his negative opinion of Whitman and showed him "the kindest treatment."[14]

Although others in the party changed their treatment of Whitman, his fellow would-be missionary, Reverend Parker, did not. The Boston minister apparently considered himself an important man, and he expected respect from the younger Whitman. Parker often was critical of Whitman. He held all of the pair's money and almost always refused to do any real work. Whitman "packed and unpacked their animals, raised the tent, and did the cooking."[15] When Whitman came down

MARCUS WHITMAN AND HENRY SPALDING

Two Suitors Ill-Suited

In the spring of 1836, two missionary couples and a bachelor-farmer—Marcus and Narcissa Whitman, Henry and Eliza Spalding, and William Gray—began their journey across the United States and its western territories, bound for the Oregon Country. There, the missionaries intended to work for the Lord and convert the western Indians. Despite their lofty intentions, this group did not represent an ideal combination of personalities. Although they shared a tent on their western trek, they did not share true friendship. The root of their inability to cooperate with one another was, quite simply, jealousy. It seems that almost everyone in the party wanted to be someone else:

> Gray . . . wanted to be a doctor and that irritated Whitman's pride.
> Whitman himself . . . wished that he were a minister; and the
> Reverend Mr. Spalding harbored a smoldering resentment at not
> having been put in charge of the overland expedition.*

To make matters worse, Marcus and Henry had a special reason to be antagonistic toward one another. The Whitmans traveled west as newlyweds. Spalding once had tried to court the new Mrs. Whitman.

Henry and Narcissa had met years earlier, when Henry was a ministerial student in the town of Prattsburg, New York, where Narcissa lived. He had fallen for Narcissa, and "had mistaken her natural friendliness for personal affection."** In love with the outgoing

with dysentery and the wagon party left him behind, Parker did not stay to help his partner. He left Whitman "and took his meals with the fur brigade's captain."[16]

young woman, Henry proposed marriage. Not having the same feelings for him, Narcissa turned him down. The rejected Henry then turned on the object of his affections with bitter emotion.

Henry went on to marry another young woman. He had not yet recovered from his disappointment and anger with Narcissa, however, when the opportunity came to accompany the newlywed Whitmans to Oregon. When approached by the missions board, Spalding responded harshly: "I do not want to go into the same mission with Narcissa, as I question her judgement."*** Nonetheless, despite his misgivings, Henry Spalding agreed to join with the Whitmans.

His decision was a probable mistake. There he was, in close proximity to the Whitmans on their honeymoon. As for his wife, Eliza Spalding was somber, ill, and humorless, far different from the lively Narcissa to whom he had proposed years earlier. Emotions ran high among the members of the party. Henry constantly criticized Marcus, and arguments flared up regularly. As for Narcissa, she sometimes felt caught in the middle. In a letter to her father, she wrote that "the man who came with us is one who never ought to have come. My dear husband has suffered more from him in consequence of his wicked jealousy, and his pique towards me, than can be known in this world."†

* Horn, 57–58.
** Ibid., 58.
*** Ibid.
† Ibid.

The party reached Ft. Laramie, in modern-day Wyoming, and then continued on to the Green River rendezvous. On this leg of the journey, the party was led by an old hand on the beaver frontier, Thomas Fitzpatrick. In the great meadow of the rendezvous, trappers, traders, and American Indians had gathered. Jim Bridger, Kit Carson, and Captain William Drummond Stewart were there. Whitman was a witness to a shoot out between Carson and a wild mountain man named "Bully" Shunar, who had challenged any and all comers. As the missionary watched, wide eyed, Carson shot Shunar in the hand after his opponent fired at him and missed.

Whitman's medical skills became the center of attention once again when Jim Bridger asked the physician to remove a Blackfoot arrowhead that had been imbedded in the mountain man's back for three years. Once it became known that Whitman was a doctor, other trappers approached him with ailments of their own.

When the time came to leave the rendezvous, it was decided that Reverend Parker would continue on to the villages of the Nez Perce because the missions board had appointed him as their representative. Whitman returned to the East to recruit future western missionaries. Parker reached Fort Vancouver on October 29, 1835. After studying everything in the Oregon Country, from the American Indians, to the climate, to the flora and fauna, he took a ship back to the East Coast. Whitman arrived home in December and took up his courtship of Narcissa. In 1836, they set out on their great adventure in the West—an adventure that brought them both not only great joy and reward, but also pain, sorrow, and early death.

Wagon Road West

By 1838, Oregon and the Oregon Trail were the objects of great debate in the United States. The western wagon road delivered fur men, traders, missionaries, and explorers into the Oregon Country, but that region of North America still was not part of the United States: It was a disputed and foreign land. With each caravan of wagons and pack animals that delivered more Americans into the Far West, however, the question of Oregon's future was discussed. The question was asked in America's churches, town halls, and taverns: Why should the Oregon Country not become exclusively American territory? To many of those who were convinced that the region should become part of the United States, the key lay in numbers. Great Britain, Russia, and the United States all might claim the Oregon Country, but the United States was the only nation in a position to people it. By the 1840s, Americans were moving into Oregon by the thousands.

MORE MISSIONARIES WEST

One of those who led the vanguard was Jason Lee, who began campaigning in the 1830s for his fellow Methodists to migrate out to Oregon. Already living in Oregon, in 1838 he took a trip back East. Leaving the Willamette River Valley, he paddled a canoe to the Columbia and then upriver. He arrived at the Whitman Mission on April 14 and talked with Marcus Whitman about his plan to deliver Methodists to Oregon. When Lee left the mission, he carried a letter from Whitman and Spalding to their missions board, requesting more than 200 recruits for their Congregationalist and Presbyterian mission work. The men asked for teachers, doctors, farmers, and others and included a list of needed items, such as tools, books, and a flourmill.

Continuing on his way east, Lee soon encountered travelers headed west to Oregon. These included a group of missionaries and their wives. When these immigrants reached the Whitman Mission, Narcissa played host, serving them "fresh milk, melons, and potatoes from the garden, and pumpkin pies."[1] The ministers then organized the Oregon Mission of the American Board. Because the missionaries' wives were not allowed to participate, the women formed their own group, the Columbia Maternal Association, with Eliza Spalding as president and Narcissa Whitman as corresponding secretary. As for Jason Lee, when he reached the East, he began a speaking tour. On it, he campaigned for Americans to move to Oregon, push the British out, and take the region as their own.

Lee gained no significant numbers of followers immediately, however. His timing was both unfortunate and fortunate. The United States had fallen into an economic depression known as the Panic of 1837. The financial slump had caused the foreclosure of many farms. Prices for farm products were poor, and farmers could not repay their farm loans. For the

The Whitman Mission (*above*) near Walla Walla, Washington, grew into a major stopping point along the Oregon Trail. It was also the site of a horrific massacre by the Cayuse tribe, whose population had been decimated by a measles outbreak brought to the area by the mission. On November 29, 1847, the Cayuse killed Marcus and Narcissa, along with 12 other settlers, and most of the buildings were destroyed.

moment, at least, many who might want to head west simply did not have the money to do so. These people also realized, however, that Oregon might be the answer to their economic woes. Lee spoke of Oregon as a promised land, a place where a civilized American could establish himself anew. Moving to Oregon cost money, however, so those who dreamed of a better life in the open spaces of the Pacific Northwest began to save what little money they could.

Others did not have to wait and were eager to make their way west. One such group, from Peoria, Illinois, formed an emigrant company that they called the Oregon Dragoons. They began to make plans to go to Oregon and drive the Hudson's Bay Company out of the region. Their leader, Thomas Jefferson Farnham, organized his people by giving them instructions to pack food for the first 400 miles of their trip. Beyond that point, the party planned to hunt wild game for food, even though no one in the party had any real experience as a hunter. Farnham's wife sewed a flag for the party. It included the slogan, "Oregon or the Grave."

The Oregon Dragoons headed west in April 1839, a party of fifteen naïve souls. Poor planning led several to drop out before the group left Missouri. In the end, only Farnham reached Oregon, but even he did not stay. After returning to Illinois, he wrote several letters that were published in midwestern newspapers. Farnham's early writings about his Oregon trek were so negative that several American parties of would-be Oregon emigrants gave up their dreams of heading west without laying a single footprint on the Oregon Trail. (In later years, Farnham changed his mind and wrote glowingly about Oregon.)

Others, of course, did pack up and follow the trail westward. One was Joel Pickens Walker, whose brother, Joseph Reddeford Walker, was a well-known mountain man. From Virginia, Joel Walker had pioneered land in Tennessee and Missouri. In the spring of 1840, he, his wife, and their five children joined a party of Presbyterian missionaries and headed to Oregon. When the Walkers reached Fort Hall, they abandoned their wagons and continued on horseback to their destination. Joel Walker and his family were among the first to reach Oregon by way of the trail to take up farming in the region.

The arrival of farmers in the Oregon Country coincided with the decline of the western fur trade, as Eastern and European fashion turned from beaver hats to silk hats. Some of those who made their way to Oregon during the late 1830s were former mountain men, such as the party of four trappers who reached the Whitman Mission in the summer of 1840. Three of the trappers—Joe Meek, Doc Newell, and Caleb Wilkins— brought along their Nez Perce wives, all sisters.

These veterans of the beaver trade realized that the day of the mountain man was over, and they would have to take up a new line of work to survive in the West. Along with Francis Ermatinger, they moved to the Willamette River Valley and put down roots as farmers. They brought their personal goods to the valley in the wagons that the Walker family had left behind at Fort Hall. Although they were forced to struggle with the wagons (they finally removed the wagon beds and tied their belongings onto the running gear), they managed to get them to the Whitman Mission. In doing so, they brought wagons farther west on the trail than anyone to date. Marcus Whitman was impressed. He told the former fur men, "You will never regret it. You have broken the ice, and when others see that wagons have passed, they too will pass, and in a few years the valley will be full of our people."[2] Whitman could not have been more right.

BOUND FOR CALIFORNIA

One of the most important emigrant parties to travel the Oregon Trail as the 1840s dawned did not hit the trail bound for the Oregon Country. Instead, they headed to California. In 1841, one of the first overland emigrant groups to reach California by way of the Oregon Trail was a party led by 25-year-old John Bidwell. Bidwell, "handsome, intelligent, and imbued with the pioneer spirit,"[3] had first moved west to Missouri. There, in 1839, he became a schoolteacher in the frontier town of Weston. He soon received a letter from an old friend, John Marsh, who had taken passage to California on a ship that followed the route around Cape Horn, the southernmost tip of South America. Inspired to move to the Far West, Bidwell spent the winter of 1840–1841 drumming up recruits for a migration to the West Coast. Five hundred excited would-be emigrants signed up and joined Bidwell's Western Emigration Society. By early spring 1841, they gathered at Sapling Grove, in modern-day Kansas, a longstanding station for the Santa Fe Trail.

Then Thomas Farnham entered the picture. Returning discouraged from his trek to Oregon, Farnham reported all his misgivings and misfortunes until the majority of Bidwell's recruits decided that Oregon was not for them, either. When Bidwell arrived in Sapling Grove, his party had been reduced to 69 men, women, and children. To make matters worse, most of those who remained were among the poorest of the group, and many were undecided as to whether they wanted to go to Oregon or to California. Among them, the members of the party did not have even $100 in cash. Some people did not have wagons. Despite these shortcomings, Bidwell set out with his party for the West.

Little went well for the Bidwell party. All too soon, the emigrants were arguing and feuding among themselves. By the time they reached South Pass, they were divided into two groups. One group had decided to go to Oregon; the other had chosen California. At the Bear River, Bidwell, 32 men, one woman, and a child broke toward the trail's left and set out for California. The only directions they had were to remain on the Bear until they reached the Great Salt Lake in modern-day northern Utah, then Spanish territory. They were to follow along the northern end of the lake and then head westward toward the Humboldt River. This leg of their westward adventure did not go well. They skirted around the lake into the desert, where they were forced to leave their wagons behind.

For a time, because the road to California was not yet well traveled, the Bidwell party lost the trail completely. By the time they reached the Humboldt River, it was late September. Food shortages began to plague the party, and they slaughtered several of their horses to survive. Continuing doggedly along, Bidwell's party finally reached California. They traversed the Sierra Nevadas and passed along the Stanislaus River until they reached the San Joaquin Valley. The party was quite fortunate, indeed. Considering that they had "no one to guide them, and no frontier experience, their achievement is one of the most amazing in American history."[4]

THE GREAT MIGRATION

Marcus Whitman saw his next wagon caravan in 1842. On May 14 of that year, a significant party of emigrants set out on the trail from Elm Grove, southwest of Independence, Missouri. The train included 18 prairie schooners, the favored wagons of those who traveled the Oregon Trail. As they set out, one emigrant woman described the wagon train "winding down the long hill, followed by an immense train of horses, mules, cattle, drivers walking by their side, merrily singing or whistling."[5] The party's leader was Elijah White, who had first reached Oregon by ship. There, he and Jason Lee had worked together at a mission. Oregon settlers had sent Lee to Washington City to lobby Congress to give support to Americans living in the region. Legislators had appointed White as an American Indian agent to investigate problems between "the natives and citizens of the United States."[6] On his way back to Oregon, White agreed to lead the party of 112 people gathered at Elm Grove.

White immediately organized the party in great detail. Believing that he had great authority as an American Indian agent and newly appointed wagon master, he gave orders readily. The party had proceeded no farther than the crossing of the Kansas River when he ordered all of the emigrants' dogs killed. Howling dogs had disturbed his sleep once too often. Reluctantly, the men of the party shot 20 dogs.

It was not long before the emigrants, tired of obeying White's orders, removed him as their leader. In his place, they selected Lansford W. Hastings. Hastings later became well known on the trail for writing an emigrant guidebook. The group never fully recovered from the awkward beginning of its trek into the West, however, and the trip remained one of disharmony and antagonisms. The emigrants broke up into smaller groups and traveled separately from one another. Fortunately, after the train reached Fort Laramie, the party hired the veteran

Emigrant parties left for unknown places in search of a better life and, possibly, free land. They were never to see their hometowns or the family members they left behind again. Before leaving their homes they saved for months, sold their land and possessions, or agreed to work for others on the trip.

Thomas Fitzpatrick to guide them to Oregon. Along the way, they stopped at the Whitman Mission. There, the party of more than 100 emigrants complained about the prices the Whitmans charged for vegetables and flour. Elijah White also delivered an important letter to Whitman from his missions board. After the Whitmans' six years in the field working with American Indians and aiding parties on the Oregon Trail, the board informed Marcus Whitman that it could no longer afford to support the missionaries' full work. The missions board dismissed the Spaldings and other, newer missionaries. The board also closed two mission stations in the region.

Immediately, Whitman and one of his associates headed for the East on horseback to plead their case to the missions board. The trip was hazardous, as Lakota war parties were said to be on the move. Whitman and his colleague rode far off the trail, dipping south into Colorado and even New Mexico. Caught in a terrific snowstorm, the missionary pair limped into Bent's Fort on the Arkansas River, a post that was located on the old Santa Fe Trail. Whitman's friend was exhausted and unable to go any farther. Whitman, wrapped in a buffalo coat, his face marked with frostbite, set out alone.

When he reached Washington City, Whitman met with congressmen and urged them to order the construction of additional protective forts in the Oregon Country. He visited New York City and spoke with Horace Greeley, the editor of the *New York Tribune*, an important and influential newspaper. Whitman convinced Greeley to support American migration to Oregon. In a rush and on a mission, Whitman, unshaven and dressed in buckskins, then met with the American Board of Foreign Missions. Through his pleadings, he convinced the board to rehire Spalding and to keep open the two mission stations the board had ordered closed.

Weary, but wanting to deliver his good news to his Christian comrades as quickly as possible, Whitman began his return to Oregon. He reached Independence, Missouri, just in time to see 120 wagons filling the town's streets. The Oregon veteran was astounded at the sight before him: "No less than 200 families, consisting of 1,000 persons of both sexes."[7] The would-be emigrants also had a herd of 3,500 cattle ready for the trail West.

To Whitman, this army of emigrants eager to hit the trail must have seemed a Godsend. Oregon fever had hit the country. An editorial in the Iowa Gazette stated as much:

> The Oregon fever is raging in almost every part of the Union. Companies are forming in the East, and in several parts of Ohio, which, added to those of Illinois, Iowa, and

Missouri, will make a pretty formidable army. . . . It would be reasonable to suppose that there will be at least five thousand Americans west of the Rocky Mountains by next autumn.[8]

Less than 15 years earlier, fur traders Jedediah Smith, David Jackson, and William Sublette had headed west with 10 wagons. Now, a massive flotilla of prairie schooners was ready to embark for Oregon. Whitman hurriedly added his name to the roster of the departing wagon train.

MISTAKES ALONG THE WAY

These pioneers made the same mistakes of earlier parties, of course. Their wagons were overloaded with nonessential furniture and other items. They took along several barnyards' worth of dogs, cats, and chickens, along with a few caged birds. They were all eager to make the trail, however. The massive caravan that came to be known as the Great Migration set out on May 22, 1843. It followed the same trail as others had before it, rolling out to Gardner, Kansas, and then turning northwest toward Nebraska. The endless prairies lay ahead, and the travelers soon got a glimpse of their first American Indians, a group of 90 Kansa and Osage "warriors mounted on prancing ponies, bearing lances, shields, and bows, their faces painted vermilion and their dark hair bristling with feathers."[9] Frightened children hid in the wagons, under their mothers' quilts.

Arguments and tempers flared early on the trek, as those who did not own cattle refused to stand guard at night over the herd. Others fought for front positions in the train to keep the dust kicked up by hundreds of wheels and hooves out of their wagons. To settle such disputes, the party chose a captain, a man from Missouri named Peter Burnett, and a group the emigrants dubbed the Council of Ten. Rules of the road were decided on. These included dividing the train into two groups, those with livestock to herd (called the "cow column") and those without.

Although the two groups did not keep exact pace with each other, they kept within supporting distance.

Although Marcus Whitman was not the leader of the party, he was approached constantly to offer advice to the emigrants. One pioneer, a Missourian named Jesse Applegate, wrote that Whitman's "great experience and indomitable energy were of priceless value to the migrating column. His constant advice was, 'Travel, travel, travel; nothing else will take you to the end of your journey; nothing is wise that does not help you along; nothing is good for you that causes a moment's delay.'"[10] Everything fell into a routine for the great double wagon train. The wagons rolled over the slight Kansas hills, where spring flowers were in full bloom. They crossed into Nebraska, where the emigrants saw their first bison tracks and prairie dog villages. The massive train was covering between 12 and 15 miles each day.

Arriving at the Platte River, the emigrants bade good-bye to the Kansas and Nebraska prairies and headed onto the seemingly endless grassy plains. Trees were limited to cottonwoods and willows along the river bottoms, and everyone collected buffalo chips—bison dung—to burn as fuel. At Cottonwood Spring in Nebraska, the party stopped to gather cedar for firewood. Here, too, the women and girls of the party did a huge amount of laundry. Despite nearly everyone in the party being a greenhorn, unacquainted with life on the trail, each emigrant was finding his or her place:

> By this time the puny found their appetites whetted by the invigorating exercise and the open-fire cooking. Antelope steaks proved more succulent than veal, and prairie-chicken stew spiced with sage powdered between the fingers was a new treat. As a fiddler scraped his violin, or the reedy notes of a mouth organ floated over the night air, babies and toddlers were hustled to bed, kettles scoured, and bean pots buried in hot coals to cook savoringly overnight. The young

The most successful groups had written rules, or bylaws, in case of disagreements. It was rare that an official, or captain, was not appointed to oversee the group while on their journey. The captain was largely responsible for getting everyone up in the morning, making sure things ran smoothly, and selecting when and where to camp at night.

people began dancing and singing; the women gossiped; the men bragged about their future plans. In an hour or so the music stilled, and all but the guards bedded down.[11]

The party moved along the Platte and then along the South Platte for 60 miles until it crossed. It then followed the North Platte. Members of the party began to feel the burdens of the trail and, once again, tempers rose. When the wagons rolled into Fort Laramie, the stop offered the travelers a much-needed break from their regular routine. They had followed Whitman's advice—"Travel, travel, travel"—and had managed to cover nearly 670 miles in 40 days.

On they pressed. They reached Independence Rock in late July, where some in the party mixed grease and gunpowder to paint "The Oregon Company arrived July 26, 1843" on the rock outcropping. As they traveled through hot weather, thick dust choked many, and insects became a burden. After covering the nearly 300 miles between Fort Laramie and South Pass, they crossed the Continental Divide and continued into sagebrush country, toward the Green River. At Bear Meadows, near modern-day Montpelier, Idaho, everyone—humans and animal alike—needed a rest. Along the banks of the Bear River, the livestock grazed in the thick mountain grass. Men and boys caught trout from the river, and hunters shot elk and waterfowl. The women and girls picked berries and uprooted wild onions.

WAGONS FARTHER WEST

The hardest leg of the trail lay ahead. The triple treats of Soda, Steamboat, and Beer Springs, in modern-day Idaho, delighted everyone. By the time they reached Fort Hall on the Snake River, however, food was running low. Then the travelers received crushing news. Officials at the fort told the party that they would not be able to take their wagons any farther on the

(continues on page 70)

FATHER PIERRE JEAN DE SMET
(1801–1873)

A Jesuit Makes His Way West

After Nathaniel Wyeth reached the Oregon Country with his party of colonizers in 1832, the majority of those who traveled the Oregon Trail over the following eight years, aside from the usual fur men and mountain traders, were Protestant missionaries, most of them from New England. In the spring of 1840, however, another type of Christian missionary reached the region: a Jesuit priest named Father Pierre Jean De Smet.

A heavyset, burly barrel of a Belgian, De Smet had come to America at the age of 20. He soon joined the Jesuit order, which had a long history of converting Indians in Canada and along the Mississippi River Valley. In 1840, Catholic officials in St. Louis ordered De Smet to head west and establish a mission in the Oregon Country. He was to minister to the Flathead and Coeur d'Alene Indian nations. Working with American Indians would not be new to the Jesuit priest. He had ministered as a frontier missionary to the Potawatami Indians near modern-day Council Bluffs, Iowa, for a decade.

That April, Father De Smet attached himself to a supply caravan heading out of Westport Landing (today's Kansas City) and bound for that year's rendezvous. It would be the last rendezvous for the dying beaver trade. De Smet soon became a favorite of the mountain men and traders on the caravan. The good padre was "short, fat, jovial, and fearless, with deep devotion to his calling and a marvelous sense of humor."* At the rendezvous, De Smet met a band of Flathead Indians who lived in the region near today's Missoula, Montana. The Flathead took him to their villages, where he tried to

explain to them "the Cross and the story of Christ."** That fall, he walked across Blackfoot lands and then paddled a canoe down the Missouri River to Council Bluffs.

The following spring, Father De Smet was back on the Oregon Trail. With him were two additional priests, three lay brothers, a carpenter, a blacksmith, and a tinsmith. The men did not travel the trail in wagons, but on mule carts, in the company of Tom Fitzpatrick's party of mountain men. That summer, De Smet and his colleagues reached Fort Vancouver in the Oregon Country. There, they met with two priests who had arrived from Canada with a Hudson's Bay Company party. Because the two priests already ran a successful mission in the area, Father De Smet and his party headed back east along the trail to northern Idaho and the Flathead nation.

During the following 32 years, Father De Smet worked with the Flathead and Coeur d'Alene nations and with other tribes in the region. He lived much as the American Indians lived, eating regional foods and riding horses bareback. Through those years of service and ministry, the good father rode approximately 100,000 miles, often across difficult and dangerous mountain terrain. So successful were De Smet and the other Catholic priests who followed in his path that Narcissa Whitman, the Protestant missionary wife in Oregon, became alarmed. She wrote: "Romanism stalks abroad on our right and our left, and with daring effrontery boasts that she is to possess the land."***

---

*Ralph Moody. The Old Trails West: The Stories of the Trails that Made a Nation. New York: Promontory Press, 1963, p. 261.
**Ibid.
*** Huston Horn, The Pioneers. New York: Time-Life Books, 1974, p. 70.

(continued from page 67)

trail. A panic ensued. There were not enough horses or mules to carry the entire party. Desperate, the emigrants approached Whitman, who told them that the wagons could make the remaining 650 miles to the Columbia River. He knew the difficulties of taking a wagon along this stretch of the trail. He was confident, however, that they would succeed better than he had because they were such a great number of people. Asking Whitman to lead them, the emigrant train came up with $400 to pay their missionary guide. Whitman accepted.

The way was difficult, indeed. Never had this many wagons rolled over the harsh landscape that led to Oregon. In the rugged, treacherous mountains, axles broke and wheels shattered. Wagons tipped over repeatedly. Emigrants rigged up block and tackle equipment to lower wagons by ropes along mountain slopes. The hooves of oxen split on the sharp rocks and left a trail of blood behind. Forty men swung axes for four straight days just to open up the route through the Blue Mountains. When snow fell on the party, the emigrants thought success was impossible. The snows melted quickly, however, and the party continued on. Exhausted, the emigrants of the Great Migration reached the mission on the Umatilla River and then the mission at Waiilatpu, one of the two missions that the missions board had ordered closed.

On October 16, 1843, after 21 long weeks of travel over nearly 2,000 miles of trail beginning in Independence, the battered wagons and their occupants rolled into Fort Walla Walla, on the Columbia River. Nearly 900 emigrants had completed the great trek, the largest wagon train in size and number to that date. Encouraged by their success, others soon followed. The Oregon Trail had become a highway.

Preparing the
Way West

Perhaps no other route in America holds more symbolic meaning for Americans than the Oregon Trail. It would play host to hundreds of thousands of people—men, women, and children—who moved west during the 1840s, 1850s, and 1860s. The incentives that existed in the America of those decades and that inspired people to pack up their lives and head out for unknown western territories are sometimes difficult for more modern Americans to understand.

For many people, the West was a great geographic symbol—an unknown to be certain, but one that might represent better opportunities ahead and that contained lots of elbow room. Although he never went west himself, New England writer Henry David Thoreau likened the urge to go to some underlying democratic urge: "Eastward, I go only by force, but westward I go free . . . I should not lay so much stress on this fact if I did not believe that something like this is the prevailing tendency of my countrymen. I must walk toward Oregon.... And that way the nation is moving."[1]

AN AMERICAN DESTINY

Americans were pulled west to the Oregon Trail because of a belief that the West was destined to be theirs. Such a view was stated most plainly by a pioneer woman who wrote in her diary:

> When God made man
> He seemed to think it best
> To make him in the East,
> And let him travel west.[2]

To other Americans, the matter was not quite so simplistic. In the minds of many citizens of the United States, the vast reaches of western lands could not be left to the "uncivilized" Indian nations or to the corrupt powers of Europe. It was clear—the word at the time was "manifest"—that it was the destiny of the United States to take its place in the West, to own all the territory from the Great Lakes in the north to the Gulf of Mexico in the south and from the Atlantic in the east to the Pacific in the west. It was an Easterner who coined the phrase Manifest Destiny to describe the tendency of Americans in the first half of the nineteenth century to envision the West as American land. John L. O'Sullivan, born in Ireland, had migrated to America to make his new home in New York City. In the summer of 1845, he wrote about this great and assumed "destiny" of the United States that lay in the West. It was our right, our duty, he said: "our manifest destiny to overspread the continent allotted by Providence for the free development of our yearly multiplying millions."[3]

Not all would-be emigrants on the Oregon Trail were driven by such philosophies. Some simply pulled up stakes from their homes back East, perhaps feeling "crowded" by neighbors

10 miles distant and itching to make their way to the wide-open spaces of Oregon. Many more were driven west, forced out by the economic depression of 1837. On May 10 of that year, just 10 weeks after President Andrew Jackson left office, eastern banks by the dozen began to close their doors. In the months that followed, wages plummeted to half, or even less than a third, of their 1837 levels. Farm prices skidded to new lows, and many farmers, unable to repay loans, faced foreclosure. The poor economy brought the wolf to many doors, and some Americans packed what little they could salvage into wagons and set out for the Pacific Northwest.

Still other Americans chose to leave their lives in the East to escape epidemics. Everywhere in the eastern United States, people died from a short list of deadly diseases that were easily spread. These included typhoid fever, dysentery, tuberculosis, scarlet fever, and malaria. Yellow fever was so common during the early nineteenth century in New Orleans and along the Mississippi River that "the regional death rate exceeded its birth rate for nearly a century."[4]

Helping to set the stage for the massive migrations of Americans on the Oregon Trail during the 1840s was a serious cholera epidemic in the 1830s. The disease first struck in Europe and then spread to America as immigrants carried it across on Atlantic passenger ships. Up and down the Atlantic Coast, American cities experienced cycles of cholera outbreaks. These epidemics continued into the 1850s. In 1850 alone, cholera killed 50,000 Americans in the East.

Even as disease, poor economic times, and an ever-optimistic American spirit pushed many into the West, some people were driven there by persecution. When the members of the Church of Jesus Christ of Latter-day Saints—the Mormons—found themselves unwanted back East, they packed up and headed into the wilderness of modern-day Utah, along the valley of the Great Salt Lake. Beginning in 1847, to get there, they followed the Oregon Trail.

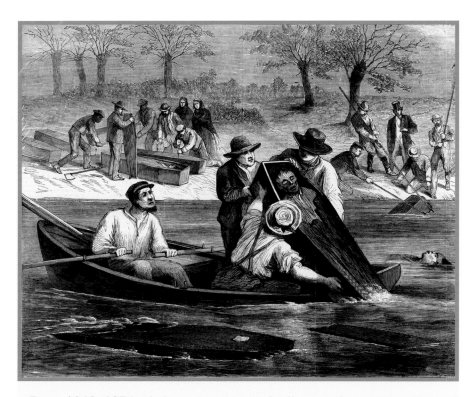

From 1849–1854 cholera was reported all over the country. Some pioneers thought they could escape it, only to be followed by it. Some wagon trains lost as many as two-thirds of their original numbers, including entire families.

"OUT IN OREGON"

The lure of western land and a generalized discontent with domestic life back East could prove a powerful incentive to a potential emigrant. It was just that for would-be pioneer Peter Burnett, who in 1853 announced to his family:

> Out in Oregon I can get me a square mile of land. And a quarter section for each of you all. Dad burn me, I am done with this country. Winters it's frost and snow to freeze a

body; summers the overflow from Old Muddy drown half
my acres; taxes take the yield of them that's left. What say,
Maw, it's God's country.[5]

The drive, the clamor to move west became so significant in the
America of the 1840s and 1850s that a popular phrase developed: "If hell lay to the west, Americans would cross heaven to
get there."[6]

With Americans looking to Oregon and its available lands
for farming and settling, the U.S. government provided a great
incentive in 1842. That year, Congress passed the Preemption
Bill, which gave permission to any American to occupy or
"squat" on a piece of land prior to that tract's being surveyed
by the government. Under the law, when someone occupied a
given piece of land and made "improvements," such as buildings
or fences, on his claim, that person would have the first opportunity to buy that property. With this law in mind, emigrants
eyed the Oregon Country, assuming that the land would one day
become part of the United States. Such an assumption proved
accurate when the United States annexed Oregon in 1848.

To many Americans, Oregon land was not just any old
land available for the taking. It was considered rich farmland.
Although the route westward crossed through less-than-
hospitable territory such as the arid Great Plains, the mountain
country of the high Rockies, and the alkali basins of northern
Utah, Oregon's Willamette River Valley was fertile and well-
watered, its climate temperate. This prevailing view of the
region is reflected in an 1843 travel book written by Thomas
Farnham, In it, he described Oregon enthusiastically: "Few
portions of the globe, in my opinion, are to be found so rich in
soil, so diversified in surface, or so capable of being rendered
the happy abode of an industrious and civilized community.
For beauty of scenery and salubrity [healthfulness] of climate,
it is not surpassed."[7]

WAGONS FOR THE TRAIL

That first great wagon train of 1843 set the stage for the thousands that followed. This 2,000-mile trek took party after party of eager greenhorns and their children across arid prairies, over rugged mountain passes, and across a seemingly endless number of dangerous rivers. It was soon realized that the nature of the journey required a special kind of wagon. The heavy freight wagons of the East—the legendary Conestoga wagons, first built in the Conestoga Valley of eastern Pennsylvania—were superior when it came to hauling heavy loads. The Oregon Trail proved murderous to these large, boat-shaped wagons, however. New designs were forthcoming.

The typical western trail wagon soon was dubbed "the prairie schooner." That popular term is derived from the wagon's white canvas covering, which, from a great distance, resembles a ship's billowy sails. New York journalist Horace Greeley described westward-heading wagon trains with this image: "The white coverings of the many emigrant and transport wagons dotted the landscape, giving the trail the appearance of a river running through great meadows with many ships sailing in its bosom."[8] The wagons' canvas coverings were treated with linseed oil to render them waterproof. Often, pioneers sewed pockets on the insides of the coverings and used them to squirrel away small items that needed to be kept handy. One Oregon Trail emigrant, Catherine Haun, wrote in her journal that "the pockets of the canvas walls of the wagon held every day needs and toilet articles, as well as small fire arms. The ready shotgun was suspended from the hickory bows."[9]

The hickory bows mentioned in Haun's journal were the curved structures that held the canvas covering up, giving pioneers about five feet of headroom inside the wagon bed. Drawstrings, or pucker ropes, were attached to both ends of the canvas top to provide privacy at night.

The wagon was built around a box that measured 10 feet long by four feet wide by two feet deep. The wagon, including

The wagons were called prairie schooners because from a distance it looked like a sailing ship across a green prairie. One wagon could usually accommodate five people. A wealthy family might have had two or three wagons, or a group of single men might share a wagon.

wheels, tongue (the pole at the front along which the animals were hitched) and all, weighed in at about 1,000 pounds when empty. It could carry, without too great a strain, between 1,000 and 1,500 pounds of household goods. The cargo weight variance was determined by how many animals (usually oxen) were used to pull the wagon. For all those river crossings on the trail, the wagon beds were caulked to make them watertight. This allowed them to float across a swollen western stream if necessary.

Such wagons were built from hardwoods, with different woods used for specific wagon parts. Wheel hubs often were made from elm or the wood of the Osage orange tree. Wheel spokes were carved out of oak or hickory. The felloe, or outer part of the wheel, was turned from ash or beech. Ash was used for the wagon box and hickory for the tongue.

In one trail guide book, *The Prairie Traveler*, written by a Captain Randolph B. Marcy, the following types of wood were suggested: "Wheels made of the bois-d'arc, or Osage orange-wood, are the best for the plains, as they shrink but little, and seldom want repairing.... White oak answers a very good purpose if well seasoned."[10] It was important on the trail to keep the moving parts of a wagon well-lubricated, especially the wheels. Each wagon carried a bucket of grease or tar, which usually was a mixture of tar or resin and animal fat.

Wise pioneers took replacement parts for their wagons with them. Out on the arid plains, wagon parts that were not properly seasoned, shrank. This caused breakdowns and delays. A wagon could break in a dozen places. Tongues sometimes snapped in two when the animals pulling a wagon pulled too far to the left or the right. On one Oregon Trail wagon train, the livestock stampeded and broke a wagon's undercarriage. The caravan's leader wrote, "Three wheels broke all to smash and 50 miles to timber."[11] With immediate repairs needed, an emigrant's dining-room table was pressed into service and cut up to make new wheels.

DRAFT ANIMALS FOR THE TRAIL

Ideally, western pioneers needed six oxen. These animals, yoked in three pairs, were rotated. Each day, two pairs were yoked together to pull the wagon. This method allowed each pair to rest for one day in every three days of travel. (An ox is an adult bull that has been castrated. Oxen are calmer and more easily trained than bulls.) Horses and mules also were used to pull wagons. Oxen, however, were cheaper to buy and cheaper to feed than horses or mules, and American Indians were not as tempted to steal them. Additionally, oxen did not require complicated leather harnesses. They could be readied to pull a wagon by hitching them directly to a wooden yoke attached to the tongue of the wagon.

In terms of purchase prices, when one group of emigrants gathered in Independence in 1852 to organize a wagon train, they found that they could purchase four- to five-year old oxen in good shape for $50 per pair. At the same time, the price of oxen in St. Joseph, to the north, varied between $45 and $55 per pair. The would-be emigrants found horses for sale at between $40 and $60 apiece and large, sturdy mules for between $65 and $75 apiece. In all, the cost of a wagon and the necessary draft animals might run between $400 and $500. By comparison, milk cows were available in Independence for $10 and $15 apiece.

Oxen could pull a loaded wagon at a constant rate of about two miles per hour over flat land. This allowed the typical wagon to cover about 15 miles per day. (Compare that mileage to a trip by automobile today along Interstate 80, which runs from one end of Nebraska to the next and follows much of the old trail route from Omaha to Cheyenne. On such a trip, 600 miles may easily be covered in a day.) Westerners understood the value of keeping one's livestock healthy. Rest periods were taken each day around noon to give man and beast a two-hour respite from the midday heat.

Although oxen were commonly used on the trail, some emigrants were not particularly enthusiastic about their performance or their capacity to survive the trail. One such skeptic recorded in his journal "that oxen are the very last kind of a team to be preferred!"[12] This veteran of the trail claimed that the most reliable animal was the mule, with horses coming in second and oxen, last. He wrote about the carcasses he saw along the trail and counted the number of horses, mules, and oxen that had expired along the way. Estimating that 3,000 mules had been used on the trail the year he traveled west, he noted that he had spotted only one mule carcass on the trail. By comparison, he estimated the number of horses on the trail at 15,000 and noted that he had seen five dead horses. He then figured that oxen on the trail might have numbered more than 80,000 and observed that he had seen between 14,000 and 15,000 oxen dead and dying along the trail.

To this statistician of the trail, oxen were not very reliable. It was rare, in fact, for an ox to complete the entire trip from Missouri to Oregon if the animal was used every day to pull a wagon. One emigrant described watching his oxen tire after months on the trail:

> We could see our faithful oxen dying inch by inch, every day becoming weaker. . . . In one or two instances they fell dead under the yoke before they would yield. . . . We found . . . that the ox was the noblest of draft animals upon that trip, and possessed more genuine hardihood and pluck than either mules or horses.[13]

Piloting a prairie schooner along a rutted prairie path took a fair amount of skill. Such wagons were rarely balanced properly; they often were top-heavy and were easily tipped over. To add to the wagons' precariousness, prairie schooners typically carried a heavy toolbox on one side and a 40-gallon water barrel on the other. This made balancing a wagon even more of a challenge. Riding on a covered wagon was understood to be something of a challenge, too. Few wagons had springs, and their primitive brakes were employed in a spirit of hopeful optimism. Emigrants sometimes dragged a log behind a wagon to slow it down when going downhill. Steering was nearly impossible: When making a turn, the outside rear wheel turned at the same rate of speed as the inner one even as the outer wheel covered more ground. This resulted in the outer wheel's skidding until it completed the turn.

PACKING FOOD FOR THE TRAIL

Not only was the pioneers' wagon technology crude, their trail diet leaned toward the basic, as well. Most pioneer families were instructed to pack the same stock of supplies. The recommended foodstuffs included largely starchy road fare. *The Emigrants' Guide to Oregon and California*, published in 1845, called for the following: 200 pounds of flour, 150 pounds of bacon, 10 pounds of coffee, 20 pounds of sugar, and 10 pounds of salt. Other commodities—including dried fruit, rice, cornmeal, chipped beef, dried beans, vinegar, baking soda (then called "saleratus"), mustard, chocolate, molasses, and tea—might round out the remaining pantry stock. Such a stockpile of foodstuffs might require between $300 and $600.

Although trail guidebooks suggested what to take on the trail and how much of it to take, the simple fact is that the foods taken west varied from one wagon to the next with great differences in between. One family from Detroit, the Richardsons—father, mother, and several older sons—packed 500 pounds of flour, 400 pounds of bacon and ham, 100 pounds of sugar, 20 pounds of coffee, 10 pounds of rice, seven pounds of tea, and a variety of dried fruits and other dry foodstuffs.

Another emigrant, a Dr. Anson Henry, packed his wagon with the following: 415 pounds of flour; 160 pounds of crackers; 100 pounds (each) of bacon and coffee; 60 pounds of sugar; 50 pounds of salt; 45 pounds (each) of apples and pickles; 43 pounds of yeast and "sundries"; and 30 pounds of cheese. In addition, he also took along 70 pounds of soap, 20 pounds of gunpowder, and 12 pounds of candles.

When the good doctor completed his trip to Oregon, he realized that he had not packed the right combination of goods. He wrote in detail about what he had learned from his personal trek west and gave the following advice concerning what foods and other items to take. As supplies for a party of 10 people, Henry suggested:

700 lbs. of flour, and 200 lbs of good butter crackers, in tin boxes, sealed up; 400 lbs bacon, hog round; 50 lbs, of lard, in tin can; 50 lbs. of buffalo tongues, or dried beef; 50 lbs salt; mustard and pepper in proportion, with as many pickles, sweetmeats, &c., as you can afford to buy and haul; 100 lbs white crushed sugar, and 5 gallons of syrup; if you omit the syrup, 150 lbs sugar; 60 lbs coffee; 6 lbs tea; 40 lbs soap; 10 lbs sperm candles [referring to spermaceti, a substance extracted from whales that made superior-quality candles]; 40 lbs of butter, put up in 8 or 10 lbs cans, sealed up.[14]

Henry also wrote about what clothing to bring on the trail, giving advice to both men and women:

Each girl should have two good linsey [a sturdy fabric typically woven of cotton or linen and wool] dresses and three good calicoes, with plenty of underclothes, (especially socks, which, bring by the dozen,) and one pair of light boy's boots, with three pair of shoes. Do not omit the boots for the females, for they will frequently have to wade half way to the tops through mud and water. Let them lay in plenty of coarse needles, thread, yarn and combs, and all the little fixings women are always wanting; and I would have all the clothing in light hair trunks, instead of sacks. Each boy should have one pair of coarse kip boots, made large, for when wet they always shrink one or two sizes, (if made wrong,) and at least two pairs of shoes made to order, if store shoes, three pair, and at least half a dozen pair of good woolen socks—two good stout suits of clothes, with an extra pair of pants, and four or five hickory shirts. Good stout box coats are very comfortable after leaving the Platte. . . . Do not load yourself down with sheets, table cloths, bed quilts, &c, but bring plenty of blankets and coarse towels. Each man should have an India rubber coat . . . and two blankets, and an India

Pictured is the interior of a prairie schooner, filled with clothes, furniture, food, and other possessions.

rubber carpet for the floor of your tent. . . . Have plenty of
tin buckets and tin cans.[15]

Keeping food edible on the trail took some doing. Eggs
were packed in kegs of cornmeal or flour to keep them from
breaking. Bacon remained edible, usually, as long as it was kept
out of the sun; it often was placed in a barrel of bran to keep
the animal fat from melting down. On the trail, coffee was the
chief drink, even for children. Pioneers told stories of horses on
the route that refused to drink western water, which was often
bitter with alkali, and drank coffee, instead. On the trail, milk
was as available as the nearest cow. Milk not drunk at breakfast
was sometimes placed in a covered pail and then hung on the
back of a wagon bed, where the day's bumpy progress jostled

it into butter by evening. Game was generally plentiful along the route, and every migrating party looked forward to its first buffalo kill.

WHERE THERE'S A ROUTE, THERE'S A WAY

Throughout the 1840s and 1850s, the vast majority of those who headed from the eastern United States to Oregon and California did so on the Oregon and California Trails. Such a trip took six grueling months. Although the trails were used during those decades by hundreds of thousands of travelers, the fact is that they were not the only ways to get to the Far West.

One way to reach the West was not by land, but by water. This meant replacing a six-month-long land trek with a six-month-long ocean voyage. The sea route took emigrants around the tip of South America and covered 13,000 miles of open water. Such a trip was not cheap. For a single passenger, the cost was approximately $300. Such a voyage often featured monotony, seasickness, and bad food. Sleeping quarters often were cramped and dirty. Ships sometimes failed to reach their destinations, falling prey to great storms. To avoid the treacherous waters around South America's Cape Horn, some people headed west by the sea route took a shortcut. After docking in a Central American port in Nicaragua or Panama, the emigrants walked on narrow trails through the tropical rain forest to the West Coast. There, they boarded ships bound for California. This route came with its own small obstacles: mosquitoes that spread yellow fever and malaria, both deadly.

A sea voyage to the Pacific Coast was not merely expensive, however. It also meant that a would-be farmer bound for Oregon arrived without a wagon, livestock, tools, or almost anything that he would need to set up a farm. In comparison, farmers who owned both livestock and a wagon could plan a trip west on the trail

Cooking on the Oregon Trail was a matter of unromantic necessity. Pioneer wives prepared their meals over open, well-ventilated fire pits, often fueled by the ubiquitous buffalo chips.

without making too much of an investment other than to buy enough food for the journey.

For the thousands of emigrants who traveled the trail, the land route was slow and tedious. Nearly everyone on the trail probably longed, at one time or another, for a quicker way to cross the treeless, almost featureless Great Plains. In 1846 and 1847, one man offered a faster wagon. A Missourian nicknamed "Wind-Wagon Thomas" built a wagon equipped with its own mast and sails. According to the inventor's claims, the sails would catch the constant prairie winds and propel the wagon along at speeds of 15 miles per hour. Such a wagon might, indeed, move faster, but it could not be steered properly, and it had a bad habit of careening off the trail into the nearest ravine.

Perhaps the craziest proposal to cross the Great Plains at great speed was made in an 1849 issue of *Scientific American* magazine. The magazine's founder, Rufus Porter, suggested a contraption that he called the "aerial locomotive," a "one-thousand-foot-long, propeller-driven balloon that could take passengers to California in three days."* The cost would be a mere $50 per passenger. Porter called for the construction of a great airship similar to those that would become reality in the early twentieth century. Some would-be emigrants signed up for the trip, but the flying machine was never built.

* Bill and Jan Moeller, The Oregon Trail: A Photographic Journey. *Wilsonville, OR: Beautiful America Publishing Co., 1985, p. 35.*

A common cooking device was the Dutch oven, which could cook everything from bread to cakes to casseroles. Cooking on the trail required much guesswork and a watchful eye. Adding to the difficulties of preparing food on the trail was the altitude factor. As wagon trains moved into mountainous regions, the high altitudes made it difficult even to bring water to a boil. Despite all of these problems, dangers, and costs (somewhere between $700 and more than $1,000 for food and transportation for the six-month trek), the Oregon Trail beckoned emigrants by the thousands.

The Way of
the Western
Emigrant

Once all preparations were made to head out west on the Oregon Trail, most families had to say good-bye to their friends and, perhaps, family members they were leaving behind. Such farewells often were heart wrenching because many emigrants knew that they might never see these people again. Oregon was thousands of miles away. When 13-year-old Martha Gay Masterson left Springfield, Missouri, with her family in 1851, their departure was a sad one. Young Martha recalled later:

> Some friends had spent the night with us and others arrived at daylight. All places of business and the schools were closed during the forenoon, and everybody came to say good-bye to us. From early morning till ten o'clock they came. The house and yard and streets were crowded with people. Friends and

schoolmates were crying all around us. . . . The sad farewells were all spoken. We took a long last look at all, then closed our eyes on the scene and moved forward. Their wails reached us as we moved away.[1]

ON THE ROAD WEST

With little variation, nearly all western pioneers bound to Oregon followed the same route. Independence, Missouri, provided the jumping-off place at the eastern end of the trail. Pioneers gathered there in early spring, waiting for the western rivers to thaw. Most travelers headed out in April, when the prairie grass was plentiful and so could provide food for the livestock. For the first two days out, wagon trains followed the old Santa Fe Trail. Then, about 40 miles due west of Independence, the emigrants spotted a crudely painted sign bearing the word "Oregon" that pointed the way. That way meant a swing to the right, to the north.

The first leg of the Oregon Trail was just about the easiest. This allowed those emigrants who were unaccustomed to working with harnessed or yoked draft animals or unaccustomed to working with a wagon to get some experience. For everyone on the trail, the first leg was an opportunity to adjust to life on the move—to get used to living in a mobile village headed west. Coming into their first stretch of American Indian territory, many emigrants kept their eyes open for trouble. There was rarely any to worry about, however. The Kansa Indians did not pose a problem for the emigrants. They were much more likely to ask people on the wagon train to trade with them than anything else. As one emigrant noted, however, "Every man displayed his arms in the most approved desperado style."[2]

About a month out of Independence, wagon trains reached Fort Kearney, in south central Nebraska, on the Platte River's south bank. By this time, the travelers had put 400 miles of dusty trail behind them. The Platte immediately struck many

Pictured is the town square in Independence, Missouri. This location was a popular starting point on the Oregon Trail and there was generally a festive atmosphere in the spring. Here emigrants stocked up on supplies, exchanged information, and assembled traveling parties.

emigrants as a river different from any they had seen before. It was alternately wide and shallow, then narrow and deep. Peter Burnett, traveling the trail in 1853, described this distinctive Nebraska waterway:

> Perhaps this is one of the most remarkable rivers in the world. Like the Nile it runs hundreds of miles through a sandy desert. The valley of this stream is from fifteen to twenty miles wide, a smooth level plain, and the river generally runs in the middle of it, from west to east. The course of this stream is more uniform than any I have ever seen. It scarcely ever makes a bend. This river has low, sandy banks, with sandy bottom, and the water is muddy.[3]

Wagons crossing the Platte usually found it shallow—a fact that surprised one pioneer, who wrote, "My first impression on beholding the Platte River was, that as it looked so wide and so muddy . . . that it was . . . perfectly impassable. Judge my surprise when I learned that it was only three or four feet deep."[4] Despite its shallowness, however, the Platte crossing was dangerous; the river bottom was unstable and shifting.

HELP FROM BISON

All along the Platte and across the Nebraska landscape, emigrant parties thrilled to the varied prairie wildlife. They began to see antelope and coyotes, as well as black bears and bison. One entertaining plains critter was the prairie dog. These little, yipping rodents lived in villages that might cover as many as 500 acres—most of a square mile. As for bison, they were plentiful across Nebraska in the 1840s. Watching a bison herd, an 1843 emigrant noted "some grazing quietly on the prairies and others marching, and moving and bellowing, and the great herds making a roaring noise as they trampled along, a half mile or a mile away. Sometimes buffalos were found among our cattle of mornings, quietly grazing with them."[5]

Bison on the trail were both a blessing and a bother. They sometimes fouled streams near the trail, leaving the water unfit for drinking or washing. Emigrants' cattle sometimes wandered off with a bison herd. Bison were considered by many to constitute good eating on the trail. As Oregon Trail pioneer Charles T. Stanton wrote, "I think there is no beef in the world equal to a fine buffalo cow—such a flavor, so rich, so juicy, it makes the mouth water to think of it."[6] Not everyone agreed with Stanton's review of bison meat, however. According to pioneer Richard Hickman, "[Bison] meat possessed the most disagreeable odor and taste of anything of the meat kind I have come up with yet."[7]

Another benefit provided by the bison was their dung, which lay scattered all over the prairie plains along the Oregon route. Dried bison dung was called buffalo chips, and the stuff made a good fuel for campfires in places where trees might be few and far between. Buffalo chips produced an odor-free flame. The chips might be collected along the trail by all members of a wagon train. One pioneer wrote, "Men, women and children are sometimes seen gathering chips—the men in their arms, the women in their aprons, and the little boys and girls will sometimes be seen carrying them on their heads."[8] It was important that the animal dung was completely dried, or it would not burn properly. Even then, bison chips only blazed in a well-built, well-drafted fire pit. They could not be used effectively in the emigrants' camp stoves. This peculiarity of buffalo chips obliged pioneers on wagon trains to develop new means of cooking on the trail. James Clyman, a mountain man–turned–trail guide in the 1840s, wrote about one such innovative and patient trail cook:

> There was one young lady which showed herself worthy of the bravest undaunted [pioneer] of the west for after having kneaded her dough she watched and nursed the fire and held an umbrella over the fire and her skillit [sic] with the greatest composure for near 2 hours and baked bread enough to give us a verry plentifull [sic] supper and to her I offer my thanks of gratitude for our last nights repast.[9]

MONUMENTS ALONG THE TRAIL

Emigrants on the trail followed the Platte River for about 150 miles. Wagons rolled along the high, flat plain between Lower California Crossing and Ash Hollow, where caravans turned to follow the Platte's north fork. With the North Platte as their guide, the pioneers kept to this river for approximately 250 miles. They then recrossed the river "just before it made a great bend to the south to its distant source in the Rocky Mountains."[10]

Moving across Nebraska territory, migrants were taught to watch for important rock formations that served as trail markers. These included Courthouse Rock, Chimney Rock, and Scotts Bluff, out on the western edge of Nebraska. When Congregationalist missionary Reverend Samuel Parker reached Courthouse Rock in 1835, it had not yet been named. In his journal, he wrote:

> We encamped to-day in the neighborhood of a great natural curiosity, which, for the sake of a name, I shall call the old castle. It is situated up on the south side of the Platte, on a plain. . . . It has at [a] distance . . . all the appearance of an old enormous building, somewhat dilapidated; but still you see the standing walls, the roof, the turrets, embrasures, the dome, and almost the very windows.[11]

Pioneers scratched their names on such landmarks, creating historical graffiti of a sort. Richard Keen, a blacksmith from Logan, Indiana, traveled the trail in 1852 and placed his name on Chimney Rock:

> We ascended about 150 feet and carved our Names [that year, Chimney Rock was estimated to be 400 feet high]. There are thousands of Names out here which will attract the attention of a man that loves to reflect and study human nature. You will see names cut a[s] high as any man could ascend you would think he leaves his Name and date above all others when probably there comes another More Ambitious than he and ascends by cutting a little higher and leaves his Name above all others . . . I ascended as far as I though[t] safe not daring to look downward but my Ambition was not sufficient to carry me any higher there is Many Names above Mine.[12]

Beyond these rock formations, the wagon trains reached Scotts Bluff, named for Hiram Scott, a fur trapper. Scott and two

Above, Courthouse Towers in Arches National Park, Utah. It is a collection of rock towers that look like a castle.

other mountain men were trekking westward along the trail when Scott became ill, approximately 60 miles west of the Nebraska bluff. His companions left him to die. The tenacious Scott continued on his way despite his illness until he reached the base of the bluff, where he died. Wolves picked his body clean, leaving little but bones. Those bones were found months later by other mountain men. Scotts Bluff is part of a break in a massive sandstone ridge that earlier travelers on the trail called Mitchell Pass. Travelers who reached the pass looked westward and spotted what many thought were the Rocky Mountains. They are, instead, the Laramie Mountains, which include the 10,000-foot Laramie Peak. The closest the trail ever came to the peak was 30 miles.

AN OASIS ON THE TRAIL

Moving on into modern-day Wyoming, the weary travelers anticipated their arrival at Fort Laramie, the site that marked one-third of the trail's distance from Independence, a distance of approximately 635 miles. Laramie was not a fort in terms of functioning as a base for U.S. military personnel. It was, instead, a trading post owned by the American Fur Company. It was one of only a few stops on that leg of the journey west, but it was one of the best forts along the trail. As described by one traveler who reached the fort in 1852:

> I find the buildings in good repair . . . the dwellings are of frame, two stories high with double porches and railings, painted white; the small outbuildings, stables, &c., are of *adobes*. There is a good blacksmith and wagon maker's shop here . . . there are also three bakeries, where the poor emigrant can obtain an apology for a loaf of bread for 40 cents, and a small dried apple pie for 50 cents.[13]

The writer referred to the high prices emigrants often had to pay in such remote trail stops. These prices were, naturally, market driven. Travelers on the trail either bought what they needed or wanted at the fort, or they did without. An Oregon Trail emigrant might pay an exorbitant 75 cents for a pound of sugar or a forbidding $2 for a pound for tea. Despite such prices, Fort Laramie represented an oasis in the Great American Desert. Here, pioneers could rest their livestock for a few days, make any necessary wagon repairs (a blacksmith was always on hand), stock up on needed pantry items, and share bits of information about local weather, river conditions, and the temperament of any local American Indian tribes.

Once back on the trail, the emigrants continued to follow the North Platte and, later, the Sweetwater River. They also found themselves in the rising foothills of the Rockies. These were the low, rough ridges that travelers called the Black Hills (not to be confused with the Black Hills of modern-day South Dakota). They were so called because the dark green cedar trees that grew along the ridge look black from a distance. After years of travel by thousands of wagons, the top of the ridge became scarred with ruts that cut into the rock to a depth of five feet. This rutted track became known as Deep Rut Hill.

Fort Laramie was a welcome site for the pioneers after the endless weeks of travel. It marked the gateway to the Rocky Mountains, and emigrants decided whether to journey on or turn back. The post trading store at Fort Laramie was one of the few places along the Oregon Trail where travelers could restock their provisions, although at very high prices. Pictured, a staff member of the Fort Laramie National Historic site stocks the trading post with items from the Oregon Trail period.

Ahead lay a great turtle shell–shaped limestone formation known as Independence Rock. Many travelers ventured off the trail to carve their names on the rock, which served as a great trail register, a custom begun by the mountain men of the previous generation. The names are still visible today. So many people "signed" the rock that in 1852, one emigrant, William Kahler, was prompted to note, even if with exaggeration, "There is at least a million names of emigrants on the rock, some are in small type and some very large."[14]

At the crest of the 8,000-foot rise toward the Continental Divide, the wagon trains moved onto a great, broad plain that stretched for miles in every direction. South Pass, "discovered" by fur trader Robert Stuart in 1812, and rediscovered in 1824 by mountain man Jedediah Smith, gave the emigrants an opening across the rugged Cordellerian mountain chain. South Pass lay at an elevation of 7,000 feet. As A.J. McCall, an emigrant who reached the Pass in 1849, noted, "We began to ascend a very gradual elevation until we reach a broad and naked plain with high, rugged, cold, blue mountain peaks to the right. The ascent is so gradual that it was difficult to fix the culminating point."[15] Here the wagon trains found the river flowing westward, a sign of their having passed into the Pacific watershed. Travelers moving through South Pass could see the Wind River Range looming in the distance, about 20 miles away to the north.

THE TRAILS DIVERGE

Here, wagons bound for Oregon could select one of two alternate routes. A shorter route called Sublette's Cutoff shaved a few days from the travel time but forced wagons to bypass Fort Bridger, as stop as necessary for some tired travelers as Fort Laramie had been weeks earlier. For those bound for California, the route to Fort Bridger was the first opportunity to turn off the Oregon Trail and set a course to California to the south. From this point pioneers could slip around the Great Salt Lake's southern shore, take Hasting's Cutoff to the Humboldt River, and pass through the treacherous Sierra Nevadas to the California promised land.

Those who stuck to the Oregon Trail soon passed the halfway point on the route, near Soda Springs in modern-day Idaho. At Soda Springs emigrants could treat themselves to tin cups and dippers of bubbly mineral water that tickled many a migrant's nose. According to one emigrant on the trail:

> The water is clear and sparkling, boiling and bubbling, swelling at times almost to the surface. It is strongly impregnated with soda, and by putting a little acid in it and adding sugar, it makes an excellent drink. It will compare with any soda

as it foams and boils up in the same way. It will also raise biscuit equal to saleratus [baking soda].[16]

On up the trail from Soda Springs, the pioneers reached Beer Springs, whose waters, wrote a traveler named Lydia Waters, "looked exactly like Lager Beer, and tasted as if it were, only flat."[17] According to some emigrants, those who drank too much water from Beer Springs became slightly intoxicated.

Up ahead lay Fort Hall, another important Oregon Trail trading post. It was nestled near the Snake River and had been built in 1834 by New England fur trader Nathaniel Wyeth. Just east of the fort the travelers had a second opportunity to make a left turn to California along the official California Trail. Those proceeding on to Oregon followed and crossed, then followed and recrossed the Snake River, well named for its torturous course. The final Snake River crossing was made at a well-established, 600-foot-wide ford. Because the water at the ford moved very swiftly, many emigrants chained their wagons together to create their own "snake" and crossed the river as a different sort of "train." Sometimes, for further safety's sake, the wagons were unloaded and the provisions floated across the river on rafts. If the Snake was raging, wagons sometimes were dismantled completely and carried across in pieces on rafts.

One hundred miles from the Snake River crossing, Fort Boise welcomed the new westerners. There was one more mountain range to cross—the Blue Mountains. There, the emigrants used pulleys and ropes to hoist their wagons over the barrier. Pioneer Helen Marnie Stewart described the process: "The hills were dreadful steep locking both wheels and coming down slow got down safe oh dear me the desert is very hard on the poor animals going without grass or water for one night and day."[18]

Two hundred miles later, the pioneers reached the mission of Marcus Whitman, and then the welcome station of Fort Walla Walla, situated on the banks of the last river leading to the Willamette Valley—the Columbia. Ahead, about all that lay in the path of the pioneers heading for their Willamette Valley paradise was the Dalles, a difficult stretch of whitewater rapids along the Columbia River. Completing their navigation of the Dalles, the emigrants floated on to Fort Vancouver, at the mouth of the Willamette River. If all had gone well, it was late October. At the end of the trail, the pioneers could reflect on their accomplishment. As one Oregon Trail veteran said, this was "Not a trip for the fainthearted; perhaps it was only for the foolhardy."[19]

THE DAY-TO-DAY TRAIL

Few of those who accepted the challenge of the Oregon Trail argued that such a journey was anything but an exciting and demanding experience. Danger and death were constantly at hand. The daily routine of westward emigration on the trail actually could become extremely repetitive, even downright monotonous. Wagon trains followed a strict schedule each day. Gunshots served as the morning wake-up call, as the night guards fired off their rifles or shotguns at 4 A.M. Campfires that had been kept alive through the night were tended anew. Soon families were rising up, dressing for the day, rounding up livestock, and preparing breakfast. A typical breakfast might include bacon, often called "sowbelly," and "slam-johns," or pancakes.

Wagons had to be ready by 7 A.M., when a cry of "Wagons ho!" called the train into motion. Often, a wagon train might stretch out to nearly a mile in length, as latecomers joined the end of the line. Each day, however, all wagons went through a regular rotation. This gave each one a turn in front, where dust was less of a problem. After covering, perhaps, as many as eight miles, the train stopped around 11 A.M. for "nooning," a midday break for people and animals alike. Women might use the time to wash clothing, while children might play or gather buffalo chips. The men might repair harness, examine the wagons, check the oxen for sore or split hooves, or discuss their progress during the morning. Lunch also was prepared and eaten. Around 2 P.M., the wagons were on the move again.

Travelers on the trail often kept going into the evening, even after dark. Once the train was stopped for the night, the wagons might be circled and chained together. Trains made up of many wagons divided into units of eight wagons, called messes, which formed individual circles. The evening meal was the heaviest of the day and might include fresh meat from that day's hunt. Evening also was the time for chores, clean up, Bible reading, and perhaps a dance, accompanied by a fiddle or harmonica. There were tasks for men and women right up to the end of each day. An 1857 emigrant, Helen Carpenter, wrote:

> Although there is not much to cook, the difficulty and inconvenience in doing it, amounts to a great deal—so by the time one has squatted around the fire and cooked bread and bacon, and made several dozen trips to and from the wagon—washed the dishes (with no place to drain them) . . . and gotten things ready for an early breakfast, some of the others already have their night caps on.[20]

Security was the watchword during each night on the trail. If American Indians had been spotted during the day, the livestock might be brought into the wagon circles. As the train's inhabitants settled for the night, guards were once again posted, often armed with shotguns instead of rifles. Any guards that fell asleep on duty—and there were many—were punished by being forced to travel at the rear of the wagon train the next day. For all of each day's effort, the emigrant covered, perhaps, 12 to 20 miles.

DEATH ON THE TRAIL

This repetitious routine could easily be interrupted by death. Disease was a constant threat on the trail, and an outbreak of smallpox or measles was a genuine cause for concern, even fear.

Dysentery was another feared and deadly disease. Called "relax disease" by the emigrants, it was brought on by poor sanitation. Dysentery caused repeated attacks of diarrhea, which in turn caused dehydration and great suffering. The most feared disease was cholera, a gastrointestinal illness. With this ailment, death came quickly and inevitably. Carried by bacteria, cholera caused its victims to experience what was called the "black vomit," often followed by shock. Anyone dying of the disease was buried quickly to avoid contaminating others. Usually, if a family experienced cholera, their wagon was quarantined from the others in the train.

There were many other ways to die on the trail, as well. Accidents were common. Pioneers drowned crossing rivers, fell off mountain passes, or were bitten by poisonous snakes. Children sometimes fell from the tongues of moving wagons and were crushed under the heavy wheels. Others were trampled by buffalo, poisoned by alkali water, or killed by lighting.

Some pioneers accidentally shot themselves. Many of the men who traveled the Oregon Trail carried firearms, even though a significant number of them were not experienced with weapons. They took guns along for personal protection or to hunt wildlife. (Little hunting was actually done along the trail in most cases, however.) A woman named Lucy Cooke, who trekked the trail in 1852, wrote to a friend, "Our men are all well-armed. William carries a brace of pistols and a bowie knife. Aint that blood-curdling. I hope he won't hurt himself."[21] Unaccustomed to carrying pistols, many an emigrant shot himself accidentally while shoving a pistol into the waistband of his pants.

All along the trail, graves marked the passage of emigrants from this life to the next. A pioneer named Francis Sawyer wrote in her diary, "Today we passed a great many new-made graves & we hear of many cases of cholera. . . . We are becoming fearful for our own safety."[22] The distinction in Mrs. Sawyer's entry of "new-made" graves is important because it told the wagon train just how near a disease such as cholera was to them. Sometimes, the presence of death preoccupied emigrants. With obsessive purpose, Maria Parsons Belshaw recorded the following entries in her 1853 trail diary:

Sept. 2	Passed 8 graves	19 cattle	made 12 miles
Sept. 3	Passed 5 graves	8 dead cattle	made 20 miles
Sept. 4	Passed 2 graves	3 dead cattle	made 17 miles
Sept. 5	Passed 3 graves	3 dead cattle	made 17 miles
Sept. 6	Passed 1 grave	3 dead cattle	made 17 miles
Sept. 7	Passed 2 graves	3 dead cattle	made 18 miles[23]

Between August 25 and September 11 in the Belshaw record, there are only two days for which no grave sightings are recorded. Quantitative studies on emigrant deaths on the Oregon Trail place the number of deaths at around 34,000— approximately 10 percent of those who set out for Oregon or California. That number works out to approximately 17 deaths per mile of the Oregon Trail.

Such records remind the modern reader that the Oregon Trail experience took a fearful physical and psychological toll on the men and women who made their way west. In an 1844 journal entry, pioneer Martha Ann Morrison makes this observation:

The men had a great deal of anxiety and all the care of their families, but still the mothers had the families directly in their hands and were with them all the time, especially during sickness.

Some of the women I saw on the road went through suffering and trial. I remember distinctly one girl in particular about my own age [13 or 14] that died and was buried on the road. Her mother had a great deal of trouble and suffering. It

Pictured is a pioneer cemetery at Chimney Rock in Nebraska. For miles emigrants were witness to the gruesome site of graveyards for those that perished along the way. One emigrant left a record having seen up to 2,000 gravesites along the Oregon Trail. Another estimated up to 5,000.

strikes me as I think of it now that Mothers on the road had to undergo more trial and suffering than anybody else.[24]

Despite popular impressions, one means of dying on the trail was rare, indeed: death by American Indian attack. Experts estimate that raids along the trail that the American Indians called the "Big Medicine Path" accounted for approximately one tenth of one percent of all deaths on the Oregon Trail; in other words, several hundred. This is a far cry from the traditional Hollywood-inspired image that many people have of American Indians riding their painted ponies endlessly around a defensive circle of wagons and picking off sitting-duck pioneers one by one.

Although the experiences that pioneers had on the Oregon Trail often appear similar, each emigrant's story is a unique account, written in personal experience. There were extraordinary tragedies such as that of the Donner Party. The Donner disaster included quarreling factions, murder on the trail, and a doomed group of emigrants trapped by heavy snows in the Sierra Nevadas. The last circumstance led some members of the Donner caravan to resort to cannibalism to stay alive until they could be rescued. The Donner drama was, fortunately, an aberration from the more usual pioneer experiences. The words of teenager Virginia Elizabeth Reed, one of the Donner Party survivors, undoubtedly rang true, however, for many western emigrants—ordinary people who wished only to survive on the trail to establish a new life in the Oregon Country:

> O Mary I have not wrote you half of the truble we have had but I hav Wrote you anuf to let you now [know] that you dont now [know] what truble is but thank the Good god we have all got throw [through]. . . . we have left every thing but i don't cair for that we have got through but Dont let this letter dishaten [dishearten] anybody and never take no cutoffs and hury along as fast as you can.[25]

JOHN C. FRÉMONT
(1813–1890)

The Pathfinder

By 1841, the Oregon Trail had already seen American traffic coming from both directions, the east and the west. This two-way flow of traffic established the route for the hundreds of thousands of migrants who traveled the trail throughout the 1840s. In that same year of 1841, however, some Americans eager to encourage the use of the trail as a route to Oregon took additional steps to further establish the route. They did this by discouraging claims that those who moved along the Oregon Trail ran a high risk of American Indian attack. One concerned politician was a senator from Missouri, Thomas Hart Benton.

Benton decided to send his son-in-law, a young second lieutenant in the U.S. Army Topographical Corps named John C. Frémont, out on a nineteenth-century version of a publicity stunt. In an effort to show how safe the Oregon Trail was, Benton convinced Frémont to take the trail west with his 12-year-old son. Frémont was to publicize this effort by writing about his and his son's adventures on the trail. To cover the costs of the expedition, Senator Benton was able to get funding from the U.S. government: an appropriation for creating a map of the Oregon Trail to America's western boundary, the Continental Divide.

Such a mapping mission was completely unnecessary, of course. The trail was well established, with no real turnoffs, and the wagon ruts could be followed by anyone. Frémont pressed on, however. He arrived in St. Louis in the spring of 1842. He brought with him a German mapmaker and a wagonload of navigation instruments and other equipment, including a large inflatable india-rubber boat for navigating western rivers. He also employed 21 French-Canadian mountain men (called voyageurs) and boatmen, who were responsible for the party's array of carts and wagons and Frémont's herd

of 100 horses. To add a bit of the legendary to his mission, Frémont hired the famous Kit Carson as his guide.

Slowed down by his preparations, Frémont and his party did not leave Westport Landing, Missouri, until mid-June. This was nearly two months later than most wagon trains departed from any Missouri jumping-off place. Nevertheless, Frémont's party might have made up for lost time had Frémont the explorer not wasted time "proving" that the Platte River was navigable. This endeavor cost the party days spent dragging the rubber raft over the Platte's endless sand bars. In all other respects, the trek to Fort Laramie went off without event.

At the fort, Kit Carson heard word of a battle that had taken place the previous spring between a group of 60 American fur traders and a party of Lakota Indians. The skirmish had resulted in the deaths of eight Lakota, and rumors were flying up and down the trail that the American Indians were on the "warpath." Carson suggested that Frémont leave his son behind at the fort, but Frémont refused. He stated that "if the [Lakota] want a battle he and his voyageurs would teach them a lesson."* When Carson shrewdly had a will made for himself, however, the French Canadians backed out of going any farther. Only when Frémont agreed to leave his son at the fort was Carson able to convince the voyageurs to continue westward.

Carson's concern about young Frémont perhaps proved true, not because of American Indian attack, but because of the elder Frémont's poor judgment. The leg from Fort Laramie to South Pass went off without a hitch, with not an American Indian in sight. Frémont and his party then began the trek back eastward. At the confluence of the Sweetwater and Platte rivers, however, Frémont made a poor decision. He decided to float back to the Missouri River in his rubber raft. He was certain that the raft would be ideal for shooting rapids. He ordered

(continues)

(continued)

the boat to be loaded—in truth, overloaded—with scientific equipment, guns, bedding, and the company's provisions as well as too many men. As Carson and several others went ahead on horseback to Fort Laramie, the overburdened boat hit the water.

At first the party found smooth sailing. When they reached the rapids known as the Fiery Narrows, however, the "overloaded craft sped [on] . . . like an elephant on a rampage."** Entering the gorge, with canyon walls towering 500 feet overhead, the raft was caught in a whirlpool. This spilled out the equipment and the party's baggage. The rubber craft "then leaped into the flying spray of the cascades."*** The raft finally pitched into the air, and the remainder of the cargo, the crew, and Frémont himself landed in the water. The men survived, but the equipment and the supplies were lost. A wet and embarrassed Frémont had no choice but to take to the trail on foot.

Despite Frémont's mistakes and miscalculations, he emerged from his trek along the Oregon Trail an inspirational figure. He wrote about his expedition, and his father-in-law, Senator Benton, ordered several hundred thousand copies of the report printed at government expense. Soon, many Americans were able to read about the trail that Frémont described "as safe and comfortable to travel as the streets of their own home towns."† New emigrants poured onto the trail in the spring of 1843, and the Great Migration of the Oregon Trail began in earnest.

---

* Moody, p. 264.
** Ibid.
*** Ibid.
† Ibid., 265.

A Flood of
Emigrants

The Great Migration that left Independence, Missouri, on May 22, 1843, set the stage for the flood of emigrants who made their way west along the Oregon Trail in the years that followed. The waves continued as 1,400 pioneers reached Oregon in 1844. That same year, wagons made their way along the California Trail, bound for the promised land of Mexican-held California. For the remainder of the 1840s, however, most of those who took the trail west were bound for Oregon, not California. The numbers tell the story. In 1845, 5,000 people in five companies emigrated to Oregon. The following year, approximately 1,350 moved to the Oregon Country by way of the trail. (The number of Americans taking the trail west in 1845 dropped dramatically largely because of the outbreak of a war between Mexico and the United States.)

With Americans moving into the Oregon Country by the thousands, the traffic along the Oregon Trail deserves credit as one of the strongest arguments in favor of the United States becoming the new power in Oregon. Great Britain agreed to reopen talks concerning its claim to the territory in 1846. The result of the negotiations was that the territory was divided along the 49th parallel. All of the territory north of that line remained part of British Canada, as did Vancouver Island, even though that strategic landmass dipped south of the 49th parallel. On June 15, 1846, the U.S. Senate approved the treaty that recognized an Oregon that was about to become strictly American territory.

FLOODING OREGON

Americans continued to flood into the region, bound now for American Oregon. In 1847, 4,500 Americans reached the region. Unfortunately, that same year was the last for Marcus and Narcissa Whitman's mission work in Oregon. After 11 years of effort at the mission at Walla Walla, the missions board had seen few conversions there. The board stopped supporting the Whitmans' work in Oregon, leaving Marcus to fall back on farming and his work as a doctor. In the fall of 1847, measles struck the former Whitman Mission, known locally as the Place of the Rye Grass. When the disease struck the local Cayuse tribe, their children died at the rate of four or five a day. Within a couple of months, measles had killed 350 American Indians, more than half the Cayuse tribe.

Despite the fact that Whitman had treated them as a doctor, many of the Cayuse blamed him and the other whites for purposefully spreading the disease. Cayuse warriors, led by their chief, Tiloukaikt, attacked the former mission in November. The Cayuse hacked Marcus Whitman to death with hatchets. Narcissa was shot repeatedly. The Cayuse then carried her out of the mission building on a couch and one Cayuse warrior lashed at her face with a riding crop. She was already dead. Ten other local settlers also were killed, including several children whose parents had died on a wagon train that had passed by the mission a few years earlier. After Narcissa was buried, wolves dug up her corpse and chewed her flesh to pieces.

THE MORMONS MIGRATE WEST

Only months before the attack at the former Whitman Mission, a unique group of emigrants along the trail arrived at their destination in the West. They had not reached either Oregon or California, however. On the hot morning of July 23, 1847, members of a religious sect that had been established back East less than 20 years earlier found themselves in the valley of the Great Salt Lake, in northern Utah. After selecting a campsite on the sun-baked plains near the lake, the men of the party took three plows and a harrow out of their wagons, hitched up a pair of faithful oxen, and began scratching the ground with furrows, intent on planting potatoes, corn, turnips, beans, and buckwheat. The temperature was 96 degrees. The ground was so hard that the iron plowshares broke. While several of the new, would-be western farmers sat down to repair their plows, others were busy damming up a nearby creek to divert snow-melt onto their barren fields. On that day, however, they need not have bothered. By the end of the day, after the men completed the plowing and planting of five acres in a hard-fought battle against the unyielding desert, the skies opened, and rain fell on the new fields. Everyone rejoiced and thanked God for His latest blessing.

These pioneers were members of the Church of Jesus Christ of Latter-day Saints. Back East, they usually were referred to as the Mormons. Their leader was a former Vermont carpenter named Brigham Young. He had led 143 men, three women, and two boys out of eastern Iowa, along the Oregon Trail, to a place in the desert that Young had personally selected. It was an unusual destination. The land lay in the northern reaches of Mexican-owned territory. The basin of the Great Salt Lake

Brigham Young (1801–1877) succeeded Joseph Smith as president of the Mormon Church. He was called "American Moses" because he led his Mormon followers through a desert to what they thought was their promised land. Besides helping to organize the Mormon religion, Young played a dominant role in the accession of Utah Territory to the United States.

was inhospitable, dry and arid; it was a place where vegetation was thin and trees almost nonexistent. As one of the new arrivals later noted, "I don't remember a tree that could be called a tree."[1] The harshness of the new environment the Mormons had chosen was exactly the point, however. Young had led this vanguard of a much larger body of fellow believers into a place where they alone might live, without outside interference and without persecution from those who did not understand them and their religion—those the Mormons called Gentiles. Just over 150 Saints had traveled with Brigham Young into the Far West. Back in Nebraska and Iowa, another 13,000 waited to join them.

A NEW FAITH

The founder of the Latter-day Saints was dead. Joseph Smith started the Mormon church in Fayette, New York, in 1830. This period in American history was rich with the establishment of new religious sects, from the Shakers to the Christian Scientists to the Seventh-day Adventists. Some of these new groups, including the Mormons, lived communally, sharing everything among their members. Because Smith's new religion stood out as unique among all others, however, many mainstream Christians rejected it. The Mormons accepted the Bible, but they also followed a new book, one that Joseph Smith claimed to have written: the *Book of Mormon.*

Smith had grown up poor on a Vermont farm. At the age of 17, he claimed to have been led by an angel named Moroni to a site on a hill near Palmyra, New York. There, he said, he dug up a set of golden tablets written in hieroglyphics that the young Smith identified as "Reformed Egyptian." According to Smith, the angel instructed him to translate the tablets. Using a special pair of crystal glasses that he said he dug up near the site of the golden tablets, Smith followed the angel's instructions.

Smith soon presented this new revelation to those who would hear his message. According to the golden texts, no existing religious group represented the true church of Christ. Smith's new revelation was the *Book of Mormon.* The book claimed that Jesus Christ had visited America after his resurrection and had preached salvation to the American Indians, who were the descendants of the ancient Lost Tribes of Israel. Jesus promised to return to North America after the "true church" was finally established. According to Smith, the angel Moroni and the book of the tablets directed him to reestablish the true church of Jesus Christ.

Soon, Smith had many followers who were ready to accept the *Book of Mormon* and live as part of this new religious sect. Within the first year of his public call to establish the true church of Jesus Christ, Smith gained 1,000 supporters. By following Joseph Smith without questioning, they were promised "their election as a chosen people who would reap the double benefits of living in an earthly city of God before inheriting the inner circle of the heavenly hereafter."[2] Smith's message was so exclusive, however, that other Christian groups responded negatively to the Mormons' assumption that they alone were among God's elect. Most of the Mormons did not care whether outsiders accepted them or not, however. They believed that they had the truth, and the Gentiles did not. The Mormons separated themselves from almost everyone else, a position that simply made them look even more suspicious to those who did not like them.

A PERSECUTED SECT

The Mormons found it difficult to live anywhere without persecution. When they settled near Kirtland, Ohio, they were criticized in the local newspapers. There, on a Saturday night in March 1832, a mob attacked Joseph Smith, tarring and feathering him. Although the Mormons remained in Kirtland for another six years, they eventually were pressured to move farther west, to Missouri. They found no friends there, either. The state's governor, Lillburn Boggs, spoke out against them, declaring, "The Mormons must be treated as enemies and exterminated or driven from the state."[3] Boggs intended to use the state militia to rid Missouri of the stain of Mormonism. Again, Smith and his followers removed themselves to another place. This time, they headed back East, across the Mississippi River to Illinois. It was at that time that Joseph Smith appointed Brigham Young as the president of the Latter-day Saints' Quorum of the Twelve Apostles.

The Mormons settled near a small river town named Commerce and began at once to build their own city of God. They named it Nauvoo, from a Hebrew word that means "a place of beauty and rest." For another six years, the Mormons prospered at Nauvoo. They added to their number until their religious settlement was 35,000 strong, making Nauvoo the largest city in Illinois. So powerful was Joseph Smith—the settlement "was his fiefdom, and he became a law unto himself"[4]—that state legislators allowed him to operate Nauvoo on his own. (With all the Mormon votes in his control, Smith, after all, could sway elections.) The Mormons even had their own militia; it had 4,000 men. The militia's muskets and swords were provided by the state of Illinois.

The days of the Mormons' Illinois sanctuary eventually ended, however. Jealous outsiders watched as the Mormons prospered. Then a secret among the Mormons leaked out. A few years earlier, Prophet Joseph Smith had received his last revelation. He had been instructed, he said, that Mormon men should marry as many women as they possibly could support. Smith did not reveal this alleged divine instruction until 1843, and then only to the church's elders.

The Mormon practice of polygamy—allowing one person to have more than one spouse—was not announced publicly for another nine years. To Smith, polygamy was a religious act. According to the Mormon church, the practice of men having multiple wives constituted "celestial marriage." The practice was related to the Mormon belief that all family members would be reunited in the afterlife. In that spiritual realm, each husband and his wives would continue to multiply, producing children in the spirit. To those who were critical of the Mormons, the practice appeared as nothing more than an excuse for Mormon men to surround themselves with multiple sexual partners. The result could only be to increase Mormon numbers through the birth of many children. As for Joseph Smith, he practiced what he preached. He may have had as many as 60 wives.

PROBLEMS OF POLYGAMY

The practice of polygamy recast the Mormon Church in the eyes of its neighbors and sparked a new wave of criticism. "Celestial marriage" was not even accepted by all Mormons. Some of them turned on Smith. They established a newspaper, the *Nauvoo Expositor*, that ran critical editorials against polygamy and against Smith's latest announcement: that he was planning to run for president of the United States. An angry Smith turned on his Mormon critics and demanded that the newspaper be silenced. Outsiders who were looking for an excuse to take action against the Mormons stepped in, claiming that Smith was attacking freedom of the press. The Gentiles soon arrested Smith and his brother, Hiram, placing them in the jail in the neighboring community of Carthage, Illinois. Then, on June 27, 1844, Illinois militiamen, disguised with lampblack on their faces, attacked the jail and shot Joseph Smith. Hiram Smith was also killed as he fought off his assailants.

The deaths of the Smith brothers sent the Mormon faithful in Nauvoo into spasms of fear. They were so worried that the bodies of Joseph and Hiram Smith would be exhumed and desecrated by the church's enemies that loyal Mormons half filled the brothers' coffins with sand and entombed their bodies secretly beneath the Mormon temple in Nauvoo. Already divided internally, the Latter-day Saints might have splintered apart. They did not do so because of the immediate actions taken by one of the church's most respected elders, Brigham Young. Young managed to patch up the ill will between the Mormons and the outsiders, and the Mormons were able to remain in Nauvoo for another year, relatively unharmed.

For many Mormons, Young was the new prophet, taking the place of Joseph Smith. (Young even married eight of Smith's widows.) The clock was ticking on the Mormons, however. Once the shock of the deaths of the Smith brothers was forgotten by their neighbors, the Gentiles began harassing the Mormons once again. In September 1845, a raid on the Mormon settlement at Lima, Illinois, resulted in the burning of 150 Mormon homes and other buildings. Young and his followers knew that they could not remain in Illinois. Once again, the unpopular sect of Saints had to move, but to where?

Brigham Young believed that he knew where. Young and several other elders had read with enthusiasm the report of John C. Frémont on his government-sponsored exploration along the Oregon Trail in 1842. Frémont had traveled and written about Oregon, California, and the valley of the Great Salt Lake. Frémont's exploration and subsequent report included so much information about the trail that Young decided that the Mormons should emigrate to the Far West and settle, not in California or Oregon, but in the Salt Lake Valley. It was a site so desolate that the Mormons would not have to share it with anyone else, and their days of persecution might finally be over. With a voice reminiscent of Prophet Smith's, Young instructed his Mormon followers:

> And from this place ye shall go forth into the regions westward; and inasmuch as ye shall find them that will receive you, ye shall build up my Church in every region, until the time shall come when it shall be revealed unto you from on high, where the city of the New Jerusalem shall be prepared, that ye may be gathered in.[5]

PLANS TO MIGRATE WEST

The Saints were going west, and Brigham Young was their Moses. Through the winter of 1845–1846, great plans were made for the migration along the Oregon Trail. Mormon men and women labored intensively, as "every house in Nauvoo was turned into a workshop."[6] Planning was the key to success, something Brigham Young clearly understood. "Prayer is good," the Mormon leader admitted, "but when baked potatoes and pudding and milk are needed, prayer will not supply their place."[7] The Mormons built and tooled almost everything they would need to make their move westward: wagons, tents, barrels, and traveling clothing. They sold their property to buy livestock, food, and ammunition. As he organized his westward migration, Young planned to advance his followers along the Oregon Trail in separate wagon caravans, with their members divided into groups of "hundreds" and "fifties." A captain would preside over each group. Using emigrant guidebooks, Young wrote out instructions for the trail:

> At 5:00 in the morning, the bugle is to be sounded as a signal for every man to arise and attend prayers before he leave his wagon. Then cooking, eating, feeding teams, etc. till seven o'clock, at which time the camp is to move at the sound of a bugle. Each teamster to keep beside his wagon with his loaded gun in his hands or in his wagon, where he can get it at any moment. . . . If you do these things, faith will abide in your hearts; and the angels of God will go with you, even as they went with the children of Israel, when Moses led them from he land of Egypt.[8]

As Young made his plans for the next chapter in the history of the Mormons, the Saints could not work fast enough. That winter, Gentile harassment was so constant that Mormon parties began to pack up and move out of Illinois. By the spring of 1846, only 500 Mormons remained in Nauvoo, and they soon were driven out by impatient Gentile mobs. The new Mormon gathering place was located in southeastern Iowa.

Driven from their homes, the Mormon parties filtered across Iowa throughout the fall of 1846. Sixteen thousand Saints made their way to a log community of 1,000 cabins that Young had ordered built along the eastern banks of the Missouri River, at a site called Winter Quarters, just west of Council Bluffs. In this western exile, the Mormons waited through a difficult winter for the spring thaws that would signal the start of their migration along the Oregon Trail. Despite Young's detailed planning, the encampment faced food shortages. These, combined with a cholera outbreak, killed between 600 and 700 of the Saints.

BOUND FOR THE GREAT SALT LAKE

When spring arrived, Young chose those among the Saints who would take up the vanguard of the Mormon movement west. He chose nearly 150 Saints, nearly all men. Young and his pioneer band set out along the trail on April 17, 1847, in search of the Valley of the Great Salt Lake. The plan was for a much larger group of Mormons to follow the vanguard later that summer. Having had their fill of persecution, the men of Young's party followed a slightly different path than was usual; they walked along the northern bank of the Platte River while the Gentiles on the trail followed the river's south bank. The pioneer band made good progress without any significant difficulties. Young provided good leadership and kept his party in line while avoiding outsiders. On the trail, Young encouraged two of his favorite activities, prayer and dancing.

The party made its way across Nebraska and into Wyoming. When the Saints reached South Pass, they encountered the famous mountain man and trail guide Jim Bridger. He expressed to Young his doubts that the Saints' plan to raise crops in the Valley of the Great Salt Lake was workable. Bridger said that the valley was too cold at night for farming. Young

Since its founding in 1830, the Mormons were treated harshly for their unorthodox religious beliefs. After the death of Joseph Smith in 1844, Smith's successor, Brigham Young, called for the Saints to organize and move west. Beginning in April 1847 and ending in 1869, about 70,000 Mormon pioneers migrated from the midwest to the Salt Lake Valley (present-day Utah).

ignored the advice. He stated, matter-of-factly, "God has made the choice—not Brigham Young."[9]

The Saints continued their westward march. After months on the trail and hundreds of miles, they discovered that their final 36 miles would be the worst of all. To make matters worse, Young became ill. He struggled with Colorado tick fever. This last leg of the venture led across a narrow, almost impassable, trail in the Wasatch Mountains, just beyond Fort Bridger. That particular stretch of the California Cutoff was a new one; it had just been opened the previous year by another pioneer wagon train, one that already had become the stuff of western trail legend: the Donner Party.

An advance group of the pioneer band reached the Valley of the Great Salt Lake ahead of Young and the main party. When they first set their eyes on the valley, they were not encouraged. Before them lay a "broad and barren plain hemmed in by mountains blistering in the burning rays of the midsummer sun . . . a seemingly interminable waste of sagebrush . . . the paradise of the lizard, the cricket and the rattlesnake."[10] One of the three women in the pioneer band was, without question, disappointed. She wrote, "We have traveled fifteen hundred miles to get here and I would willingly travel a thousand miles farther to get where it looked as though a white man could live."[11]

The Valley had always been Young's intended destination, however, and he was intent on turning it into a Mormon paradise. The Salt Lake would be their neighbor. The Gentiles would eternally keep their distance. The Mormons would make themselves a home. With a deep faith and a determined heart, Young assured his followers that they had landed exactly where Providence intended: "We have been thrown like a stone from a sling and we have lodged in the godly place where the Lord wants his people to gather. . . . If the Lord should say by His revelation this is the spot, the Saints would be satisfied if it was a barren rock."[12] That first day in the valley did not end until the potatoes were planted in the ground.

THE ENDURING LEGACY OF THE TRAIL

On August 14, 1848, Congress passed a bill creating the Territory of Oregon. The following March, a territorial government was established, and the territory's first governor was chosen. By then, gold had been discovered in California, and emigrants

(continues on page 122)

THE SAINTS' DESERT PARADISE

Mormon elder Brigham Young reached the Salt Lake Valley with an initial party of fewer than 150 Saints, but others soon followed. In time, the world created in the remote lands of Young's choosing established, not only the Mormon faith in the desert, but also American civilization, as well.

Hundreds followed immediately in the wake of the pioneer band led by Young. As the Mormon leader made his way back east along the trail, he greeted hundreds of fellow Mormons who had set out from Winter Quarters in Iowa for the Great Salt Lake. Young gave them encouragement. He told them that their fellow Saints had already planted crops to provide them with food. The first year or so proved difficult, however, for all those who tried to make modern-day northern Utah their home. Only through cooperation and communal living were the Saints able to tame the valley and make it theirs. By 1849, just two years after Young's arrival in the Valley of the Great Salt Lake, the region was home to more than 5,000 Saints. Although Young credited God with the success of the Mormon colony, nothing had a greater impact on the sect's livelihood in the Far West than the California Gold Rush, which began drawing thousands to northern California in 1849. Would-be prospectors who traveled the Oregon Trail passed through Salt Lake City. This proved to be a boon to the Mormon economy. By the time of the Gold Rush, the United States had defeated Mexico in a war that brought about the handoff of the northern Mexican provinces as U.S. territory, the area including the region occupied by the Mormons. In 1850, the Utah Territory was established.

Throughout the 1850s, Mormons flooded along the Oregon Trail into the Valley of the Great Salt Lake. They came not only from the eastern United States, but also from Europe. Between 1856 and

1860, approximately 3,000 European Mormons migrated to the United States and walked the 1,300 miles from Iowa to the desert settlement of the Saints.

Many of those who came to America bound for the Valley of the Great Salt Lake were provided only with handcarts, not wagons, to haul their household goods along the Oregon Trail. A crop failure in the mid-1850s drastically cut Mormon funds for wagons and oxen. The first party to reach the Utah colony by handcart came in 1856. The carts were built in Iowa City by Mormon craftsmen and were little more than squarish wooden boxes flanked by two large wheels. The Saints were required to pull the carts by hand, a difficult task for those traveling the Oregon Trail. By 1856, more than 60,000 Mormons had traveled the length of the Oregon Trail.

Success came to the Mormon settlement around the Great Salt Lake. Young's order to his people was industry: "Produce what you consume."* He oversaw the construction of everything from gristmills to sawmills to ironworks to tanneries. By 1853, "Salt Lake City hummed with the manufacture of flannels, linseys, jeans, pottery and cutlery."** That same year, the Saints broke ground for the construction of a great temple, a massive granite building built from materials carved out a stone quarry 20 miles away from Salt Lake City. The temple took 40 years to construct. Brigham Young did not live to see its completion, however. He died in 1877, 16 years before the great Mormon temple was finished.

---

* Horn, p. 176.
** Ibid.

(continued from page 119)

were drawn to the trail as never before. Thirty thousand people reached the gold camps of northern California in 1849. The following year, another 55,000 came. That year, 1850, saw the largest number of travelers on the Oregon Trail. At Fort Laramie, which had become an official army post in 1849, soldiers kept exact records of nearly everything that moved that reached the fort. The statistics for 1850 tell the story: 8,998 wagons, 7,472 mules, 30,616 oxen, 22,742 horses, and 5,270 cows. The following year—1851—the U.S. Army negotiated a treaty with several American Indian nations, including the Lakota, Cheyenne, Arapaho, Snake, and Crow. This treaty granted permission for non-American Indians to construct additional forts along the Oregon Trail. The year 1852 delivered another 40,000 emigrants along the western trail.

The westward migrations continued throughout the 1850s and 1860s. Pioneer wagon trains filled with would-be western farmers made up the vast majority of those who traveled the trail. At the same time, other travelers also used the great western road for other purposes, just as the mountain men and fur traders had used the trail back in the 1820s and 1830s. By the 1850s, freight wagons rolled along the trail in large numbers, their owners having contracted with the federal government to deliver supplies and mail to remote trail forts and army posts. By then, the heyday of the Oregon Trail had passed, however. By 1855, the California Gold Rush had died down, and the trail saw smaller numbers of westward travelers. Civilization was bound for the West. In 1854, Congress passed the Kansas-Nebraska Act, which opened up western lands to further settlement. In 1869, the transcontinental railroad was completed. The railroad followed much of the Oregon and California trails. By that year, at least 350,000 hearty souls had traveled from the East to the West on these two trails.

DISCOVERING TODAY'S TRAIL

Today, the Oregon Trail is remembered as one of the most important western routes in American history. Although wagons no longer travel the trail from Nebraska, to Wyoming, to Idaho, and beyond, much of the old trail can be followed today by car or train. Modern highways parallel the old wagon trail, allowing drivers and their passengers to cover hundreds of miles in a day—distances that would have been unfathomable to a nineteenth-century pioneer. Where fur companies delivered trade goods to the mountain men's annual rendezvous in the early 1800s, long trains now deliver freight to the West and the East.

Although the trail has largely vanished from modern experience, some vestiges of the past are still visible. Wagon ruts can still be seen, 150 years after the wagons stopped rolling west. In Nebraska, people in search of the trail can find such ruts at Rock Creek Station State Park, in the southeastern portion of the state, and at California Hill, west of Brule. Outside Guernsey, Wyoming, other wagon ruts remain, cut five feet deep in the region's soft sandstone. Near Interstate 84, southeast of Boise, Idaho, the ruts remain at Bonneville Point.

The names of yesteryear's pioneers can still be read, as well. At Wyoming's Register Cliff and Independence Rock, outside Casper, visitors can still find the signatures of the past etched in solid rock. All along the former Oregon Trail, historic sites have been restored—places where the historically curious may stop and take in the ambience of the trail. These include Nebraska's Fort Kearny State Historical Park, Wyoming's Fort Laramie National Historic Site, and Idaho's Fort Hall and Fort Boise.

Yet, the past remains the past. Signatures carved in rock, reconstructed forts, and wagon ruts cut out of stone at best provide signposts along the old trail. What can never be relived is the excitement of the trail, the fever that drew hundreds of

As the emigrants traveled and paused for breaks, they would carve their names and dates of passage in the rocks. Register Rock, located along the Oregon Trail in Idaho, was a famous stopping place during the journey west. Today, the rock is protected by a weather shelter and it is against the law to leave behind graffiti.

thousands of eager Americans and others from their former homes to a place where their dreams awaited—visions of lives recast by time and distance, of worlds that lay at the end of a pioneer's vision, of places reached only through difficulty, sweat, and endurance, on a route known as the Oregon Trail.

Chronology

1700s	British fur agents arrive along the Columbia River in the Oregon Country to establish trading posts.
1792	American sea captain Robert Gray sails up the mouth of the Columbia River and claims the region for the United States.
1805–1806	The Lewis and Clark Expedition (the Corps of Discovery) reaches Oregon by land from the United States.
1811	John Jacob Astor establishes an American trading post in the Oregon Country.
1812–1813	Astor's partner, Duncan McDougall, dispatches a party of men, led by Robert Stuart, overland and eastbound. The group blazes the route that became known as the Oregon Trail. Although the group "discovers" a break in the Rockies called South Pass, the discovery is forgotten for a decade.
1823–1824	Fur-trade organizer William Ashley, along with mountain man Jedediah Smith, takes a party of trappers along the trail from east to west, rediscovering South Pass.
1825–1826	Smith and Ashley lead the first wagon parties along the Oregon Trail and through South Pass.
1827	The United States and Great Britain renew their 1818 agreement to occupy the Oregon Country jointly.
1829	Easterner Hall Jackson Kelley organizes a missionary society to take the Gospel to western Indians. His plans never come to fruition.

1832 U.S. Army captain Benjamin Bonneville succeeds in taking wagons along the Oregon Trail as far west as Wyoming's Green River. That same year, Nathaniel Wyeth successfully leads a wagon party of would-be Oregon colonizers along the Oregon Trail. His party becomes the first permanent settlement of colonizers along Oregon's Willamette River.

1834 Methodist minister Jason Lee and a party of missionaries take the Oregon Trail west and establish a mission in Oregon. Lee encourages the emigration of women to the Oregon mission.

1836 Missionaries Marcus and Narcissa Whitman and Henry and Eliza Spalding take the Oregon Trail west

TIMELINE

1792
American sea captain Robert Gray sails up the mouth of the Columbia River and claims the region for the United States

1825–1826
Smith and Ashley lead the first wagon parties along the Oregon Trail and through South Pass

1836
Marcus and Narcissa Whitman and Henry and Eliza Spalding take the Oregon Trail west with wagons and settle in the Walla Walla district of the Oregon Country

1792 — 1840

1811
John Jacob Astor establishes an American trading post in the Oregon Country

1812–1813
Robert Stuart blazes the route that became known as the Oregon Trail

1832
Nathaniel Wyeth successfully leads a wagon party of would-be Oregon colonizers along the Oregon Trail. His party becomes the first permanent settlement of colonizers along Oregon's Willamette River

1840
A Catholic Jesuit priest, Father Pierre Jean De Smet, takes the Oregon Trail west and establishes a mission in the Oregon Country

with wagons and settle in the Walla Walla district of the Oregon Country. Narcissa Whitman and Eliza Spalding become the first pioneer women to travel the Oregon Trail.

1839   Organizer Thomas Jefferson Farnham organizes his Oregon Dragoons, an emigrant party of Americans, to go west to Oregon. Many drop out, and, although Farnham reaches Oregon, he does not remain. He returns east.

1840   A Catholic Jesuit priest, Father Pierre Jean De Smet, takes the Oregon Trail west and establishes a mission in the Oregon Country.

1843
A wagon train of nearly 1,000 emigrants, known as the "Great Migration," follows the Oregon Trail to the Willamette River in the Oregon Country

1847
The first party of Mormons, led by Brigham Young, migrates along the trail to the Valley of the Great Salt Lake

1850
The Oregon Trail witnesses its largest number of emigrants: 55,000

1869
The Transcontinental Railroad is completed. The rail line follows much of the route of the Oregon Trail

1841

1869

1841
John Bidwell leads one of the first emigrant groups to reach California by way of the Oregon Trail

1846
The United States and Great Britain negotiate an agreement that divides the Oregon Country along the 49th parallel and grants the United States exclusive ownership south of the line

1848
The U.S. Congress passes a bill creating the Territory of Oregon

1841   John Bidwell leads one of the first emigrant groups to reach California by way of the Oregon Trail.

1842   The U.S. Congress passes the Preemption Bill, which gives permission to any American to occupy or "squat" on a piece of land prior to that tract's being surveyed by the government. The law encourages Americans to move to the Oregon Country. That year, U.S. Army Second Lieutenant John C. Frémont leads a government exploration party along the Oregon Trail. His reports encourage Americans to go West on the trail.

1843   A wagon train of nearly 1,000 emigrants, known as the "Great Migration," follows the Oregon Trail to the Willamette River in the Oregon Country.

1844   Approximately 1,400 Americans follow the Oregon Trail to the Oregon Country.

1845   Five thousand Americans emigrate westward along the Oregon Trail.

1846   The United States and Great Britain negotiate an agreement that divides the Oregon Country along the 49th parallel and grants the United States exclusive ownership south of the line.

1847   The first party of Mormons, led by Brigham Young, migrates along the trail to the Valley of the Great Salt Lake. Marcus and Narcissa Whitman are murdered by Indians at their former Oregon mission.

1848   The U.S. Congress passes a bill creating the Territory of Oregon.

1849   The Oregon Trail is crowded with emigrants headed to California in search of gold. In all, more than 30,000 travel the trail.

1850   The Oregon Trail witnesses its largest number of emigrants: 55,000.

1854   Congress passes the Kansas-Nebraska Act, which opens up much of the land along the Oregon Trail for settlement.

1869   The Transcontinental Railroad is completed. The rail line follows much of the route of the Oregon Trail.

NOTES

CHAPTER 1

1. Huston Horn, *The Pioneers.* New York: Time-Life Books, 1974, 54.
2. Ibid.
3. Martin T. Place, *Westward on the Oregon Trail.* New York: American Heritage Publishing Co., 1962, 65.
4. Moody, Ralph. *The Old Trails West: The Stories of the Trails that Made a Nation.* New York: Promontory Press, 1963, 257.
5. Place, 67.
6. Moody, 257.
7. Ibid., 258.
8. Place, 67.
9. Moody, 258.
10. Horn, 58.
11. Place, 67.
12. Moody, 259.
13. Ibid.
14. Horn, 58.
15. Ibid.
16. Place, 70.
17. Horn, 61.
18. Ibid., 61, and John A. Hawgood, *America's Western Frontiers: The Exploration and Settlement of the Trans-Mississippi West.* New York: Alfred A. Knopf, 1967, 147.
19. Moody, 259.
20. Place, 71.
21. Horn, 61.
22. Ibid.
23. Ibid.
24. Ibid.
25. Ibid.

CHAPTER 2

1. Place, 32.
2. Ibid.
3. Ibid., 33.
4. Ibid.
5. Ibid., 36.
6. Ibid.
7. Ibid., 39.
8. Ibid., 42.
9. Ibid., 45.

CHAPTER 3

1. Place, 49.
2. Ibid., 51.
3. Ibid., 53.
4. Ibid., 58.
5. Ibid.
6. Horn, 46.
7. Ibid.
8. Ibid.

CHAPTER 4

1. Horn, 46.
2. Ibid.
3. Ibid., 48.
4. Ibid., 48–49.
5. Ibid., 49.
6. Place, 59.
7. Horn, 49.
8. Place, 62.
9. Horn, 52.
10. Ibid.
11. Moody, 257.
12. Place, 62.
13. Horn, 52.
14. Place, 64.
15. Ibid.
16. Horn, 54.

CHAPTER 5

1. Place, 75.
2. Ibid.
3. Moody, 270.
4. Ibid., 271.
5. Place, 78.
6. Ibid., 79.
7. Ibid., 86.
8. Ibid.
9. Ibid.
10. Ibid., 89.
11. Ibid., 91.

CHAPTER 6

1. Horn, 24.
2. Ibid.
3. Tim McNeese and Michael S. Mountjoy, *History in the Making: Sources and Essays of America's Past, Volume I*. New York: American Heritage, 1994, 265.
4. Horn, 25.
5. McNeese, 303.
6. Horn, 24.
7. Thomas J. Farnham, *Travels in the Great Western Prairies, the Anahuac and Rocky Mountains, and in the Oregon Territory*. New York: Da Capo Press, 1973, 315.
8. Paden, Irene D. *The Wake of the Prairie Schooner*. New York: Macmillan, 1947, 63.
9. Lillian Schlissel, *Women's Diaries of the Westward Journey*. New York: Schocken, 1982, 19–20.
10. Randolph B. Marcy, *The Prairie Traveler: A Hand-Book for Overland Expeditions*. Williamstown, MA: Corner House, 1968, 26.
11. Horn, 88.
12. Herbert Eaton, *The Overland Trail to California in 1852*. New York: G.P. Putnam's Sons, 1974, 4.
13. James Hewitt, ed. *Eye-Witnesses to Wagon Trains West*. New York: Scribner's, 1973, 48.
14. Eaton, 9.
15. Ibid.

CHAPTER 7

1. Gary L. Blackwood, *Life on the Oregon Trail*. San Diego: Lucent Books, 1999, 23.
2. Barton, Lois, ed. *One Woman's West: Recollections of the Oregon Trail and Settling the Northwest Country by Martha Gay Masterson 1838–1916*. Eugene, OR: Spencer Butte Press, 1986, 12.
3. Horn, 92.
4. McNeese, 305.
5. Horn, 93.
6. Eaton, 159.
7. Joel Palmer, *Journal of Travels over the Rocky Mountains*. Ann Arbor, MI: University Micro-films, 1966.
8. Eaton, 88.
9. Horn, 93.
10. Moeller, 46.
11. Marc Simmons, et al. *Trails West*. Washington, D.C.: National Geographic Society, 1979, 59.
12. Ibid.
13. Blackwood, 90.
14. Moeller, 69.
15. Ibid., 72.
16. Ibid., 86.
17. Ibid.
18. McNeese, 306.
19. Ibid., 307.
20. Schlissel, 78.
21. Susan G. Butruille, *Women's Voices from the Oregon Trail*.

Boise, ID: Tamarack Books, 1993, 57.

22. McNeese, 307.
23. Ibid., 308.
24. Ibid.
25. Ibid.

CHAPTER 8

1. Horn, 59.
2. Ibid., 163.
3. Ibid., 166.
4. Ibid., 167.
5. Ward, 103.
6. Horn, 170.
7. Ward, 103.
8. Ibid., 103–104.
9. Ibid., 104.
10. Ibid., 106.
11. Ibid.
12. Ibid.

BIBLIOGRAPHY

Barton, Lois, ed. *One Woman's West: Recollections of the Oregon Trail and Settling the Northwest Country by Martha Gay Masterson 1838–1916*. Eugene, Ore.: Spencer Butte Press, 1986.

Blackwood, Gary L. *Life on the Oregon Trail*. San Diego: Lucent Books, 1999.

Brown, Dee. *The Gentle Tamers: Women of the Old Wild West*. New York: G.P. Putnam's Sons, 1958.

Butruille, Susan G. *Women's Voices from the Oregon Trail*. Boise, Id.: Tamarack Books, 1993.

Eaton, Herbert. *The Overland Trail to California in 1852*. New York: G.P. Putnam's Sons, 1974.

Farnham, Thomas J. *Travels in the Great Western Prairies, the Anahuac and Rocky Mountains, and in the Oregon Territory*. New York: Da Capo Press, 1973.

Gilbert, Bil. *The Trailblazers*. New York: Time-Life Books, 1973.

Hannon, Jessie Gould. *The Boston-Neweton Company Venture: From Massachusetts to California in 1849*. Lincoln, Neb.: University of Nebraska Press, 1969.

Hawgood, John A. *America's Western Frontiers: The Exploration and Settlement of the Trans-Mississippi West*. New York: Alfred A. Knopf, 1967.

Hewitt, James, ed. *Eye-Witnesses to Wagon Trains West*. New York: Scribner's, 1973.

Horn, Huston. *The Pioneers*. New York: Time-Life Books, 1974.

Marcy, Randolph B. *The Prairie Traveler: A Hand-Book for Overland Expeditions.* Williamstown, Mass.: Corner House, 1968.

McNeese, Tim, and Michael S. Mountjoy. *History in the Making: Sources and Essays of America's Past, Volume I.* New York: American Heritage, 1994.

Moeller, Bill and Jan. *The Oregon Trail: A Photographic Journey.* Wilsonville, Ore.: Beautiful America Publishing Co., 1985.

Moody, Ralph. *The Old Trails West: The Stories of the Trails that Made a Nation.* New York: Promontory Press, 1963.

Paden, Irene D. *The Wake of the Prairie Schooner.* New York: Macmillan, 1947.

Palmer, Joel. *Journal of Travels over the Rocky Mountains.* Ann Arbor, Mich.: University Microfilms, 1966.

Place, Marian T. *Westward on the Oregon Trail.* New York: American Heritage Publishing Co., 1962.

Schlissel, Lillian. *Women's Diaries of the Westward Journey.* New York: Schocken, 1982.

Simmons, Marc, et al. *Trails West.* Washington, D.C.: National Geographic Society, 1979.

Unruh, John D. *The Plains Across: The Overland Emigrants and the Trans-Mississippi West, 1840–60.* Urbana: University of Illinois Press, 1982.

Ward, Geoffrey. *The West: An Illustrated History.* Boston: Little, Brown and Company, 1996.

Further Reading

BOOKS

Burger, James P. *Oregon Trail*. New York: Rosen Publishing Group, 2003.

Fisher, Leonard. *Oregon Trail*. New York: Holiday House, 1990.

Isaacs, Sally Senzell. *Life on the Oregon Trail*. Portsmouth, N.H.: Heinemann, 2000.

Jaffe, Elizabeth D. *Oregon Trail*. Mankato, Minn.: Coughlan Publishing, 2000.

Kudlinski, Kathleen V. *Facing West: A Story of the Oregon Trail*. New York: Penguin Young Readers Group, 1996.

Landau, Elaine. *Oregon Trail*. New York: Children's Press, 2006.

Levine, Ellen. *If You Traveled West in a Covered Wagon*. New York: Scholastic, 1992.

Olson, Steven P. *Oregon Trail*. New York: Rosen Publishing Group, 2004.

Pelta, Kathy. *Trails to the West: Beyond the Mississippi*. Austin: Raintree Steck-Vaughn Publishers, 1998.

Senzell, Sally. Oregon Trail. Portsmouth, N.H.: Heinemann Library, 2003.

Woodruff, Elvira, *Dear Levi: Letters from the Overland Trail*. New York: Random House Children's Books, 1998.

WEB SITES

End of the Oregon Trail Interpretive Center

http://www.endoftheoregontrail.org/joomlaeotic/

History Globe: The Oregon Trail

http://www.historyglobe.com/ot/otmap1.htm

The National Park Service: Oregon Trail

http://www.nps.gov/archive/fola/oregon.htm

The Oregon Territory and Its Pioneers

http://www.oregonpioneers.com/ortrail.htm

The Oregon Trail

http://www.isu.edu/~trinmich/Oregontrail.html

U.S. Department of the Interior Bureau of Land Management

http://www.blm.gov/or/oregontrail/

PHOTO CREDITS

INDEX

About the Author

TIM McNEESE lives on a cutoff route of the Oregon Trail, where he is associate professor of history at York College in York, Nebraska. He is in his seventeenth year of college instruction. Professor McNeese earned an associate of arts degree from York College, a bachelor of arts in history and political science from Harding University, and a master of arts in history from Missouri State University. A prolific author of books for elementary, middle and high school, and college readers, McNeese has published more than 90 books and educational materials during the past 20 years, on everything from the civil rights movement to Spanish painters. His writing has earned him a citation in the library reference work, *Contemporary Authors* and multiple citations in *Best Books for Young Teen Readers.* In 2006, McNeese appeared on the History Channel program *Risk Takers, History Makers: John Wesley Powell and the Grand Canyon.* He was a faculty member at the 2006 Tony Hillerman Writers Conference in Albuquerque, where he lectured on American Indians of the Southwest. His wife, Beverly, is an assistant professor of English at York College. They have two married children, Noah and Summer, and three grandchildren, Ethan, Adrianna, and Finn. Tim and Bev sponsored study trips for college students on the Lewis and Clark Trail in 2003 and 2005 and to the American Southwest in 2008. Feel free to contact Professor McNeese at tdmcneese@york.edu.